# Lots of Scraps
## It's Time to Quilt™

Edited by JEANNE STAUFFER & SANDRA L. HATCH

HOUSE of
WHITE
BIRCHES
PUBLISHERS
SINCE 1947

# Lots of Scraps
## It's Time to Quilt™

Editors Jeanne Stauffer, Sandra L. Hatch
Art Director Brad Snow
Publishing Services Director Brenda Gallmeyer

Managing Editor Dianne Schmidt
Assistant Art Director Nick Pierce
Copy Supervisor Michelle Beck
Copy Editors Nicki Lehman, Judy Weatherford
Technical Artist Connie Rand

Graphic Arts Supervisor Ronda Bechinski
Book Design Nick Pierce
Graphic Artists Erin Augsburger, Joanne Gonzalez
Production Assistants Marj Morgan, Judy Neuenschwander

Photography Supervisor Tammy Christian
Photography Matthew Owen
Photo Stylist Tammy Steiner

Printed in China
First Printing: 2008
Library of Congress Number: 2007936089
Hardcover ISBN: 978-1-59217-206-1
Softcover ISBN: 978-1-59217-228-3

Every effort has been made to ensure the accuracy and completeness of the instructions in this book.
However, we cannot be responsible for human error or for the results when using materials other than
those specified in the instructions, or for variations in individual work.

DRGbooks.com

123456789

# Welcome

Early American pioneers collected all the fabric scraps left over from stitching their clothes, even the tiny pieces, and pieced them together to make bedcovers for their families. Nothing was wasted.

Today we quilters follow in that same tradition, saving scraps from past quilting projects and collecting them in boxes and bags until we are finally ready to start a scrap project. Like the quilters of yesterday, our scraps come in a variety of sizes and shapes. Many of our scrap quilts today are planned scrap quilts with the careful placement of lights and darks, or with scraps of the same color family used in a consistent way in each block.

Then there are the truly scrappy quilts like those found in the first chapter of this book. These super-scrappy quilts have no planned placement of color, and they use literally hundreds of fabric scraps. If you want to make one of these quilts and find that you need more scraps, we recommend you buy fat quarters to add to your collection. If you really want to reduce greatly the number of fabric scraps in your collection, stitch one of these quilts.

For those of you who would like to make a scrap quilt that is a little less daunting, look for the chapters containing holiday and special-occasion quilts, baby quilts, full-size bed quilts and quilts celebrating nature. All are made using scraps of one size or another.

In addition to quilts, we've included a chapter of table runners and projects for decorating your home and a collection of patchwork bags made with scraps. There is definitely something for everyone who wants to try their hand at scrap quilting. Just select your first project, and you're on your way to hours of scrap quilting enjoyment.

Happy quilting!

*Jeanne Stauffer*

*Sandra L. Hatch*

# Contents

# Super-Scrappy Quilts

Don't let the number of scraps used in these quilts keep you from making one that you admire. Spend as little as 30 minutes at a time rotary-cutting your scraps into the right size of squares or shapes that you need. You'll be surprised at how quickly you'll have all the pieces cut. Spend the same 30 minutes at a time sewing, and you'll soon have a quilt that you will treasure and pass down to the next generation.

# 36-Patch Scrappy

Design by SANDRA L. HATCH

The background squares in this quilt were created with light-color scraps and a few dark ones thrown in for good measure. Collect squares from all of your quilting buddies to expand your stash for use in this design.

## Project Specifications

Skill Level: Intermediate
Quilt Size: 96" x 112"
Block Size: 16" x 16"
Number of Blocks: 20

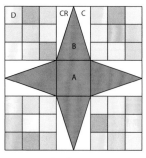

**36-Patch Scrappy**
16" x 16" Block
Make 20

| FABRIC<br>Measurements based on 42" usable fabric width. | #STRIPS & PIECES | CUT | #PIECES | SUBCUT |
|---|---|---|---|---|
| Assorted light scraps | 892 | 2½" D squares | | |
| ¾ yard salmon tonal | 11 | 2¼" x 42" binding | | |
| 2 yards cream tonal | 7 | 6½" x 42" | 240 | C & CR pieces as directed in Special Cutting Instructions |
| | 8 | 2½" x 42" E/F | | |
| 5¼ yards rose print | 3 | 4½" x 42" | 20 | 4½" A squares |
| | 6 | 6½" x 42" | 120 | B pieces as directed in Special Cutting Instructions |
| | 8 | 4½" x 42" G/H | | |
| | 10 | 8½" x 42" I | | |
| Backing | | 102" x 118" | | |

### SUPPLIES

- Batting 102" x 118"
- All-purpose thread to match fabrics
- Quilting thread
- Basic sewing tools and supplies

## Special Cutting Instructions

**Step 1.** Prepare templates for B and C pieces using patterns given.

**Step 2.** Cut B pieces as directed from the B strips as shown in Figure 1.

**Figure 1**

**Step 3.** Fold the C strips with right sides together to make 6½" x 21" strips. Cut the C and

CR pieces from the strips at one time through the folded strips as shown in Figure 2.

**Figure 2**

## Completing the Blocks

**Step 1.** Select nine D squares; join three squares to make a row. Press seams to one side. Repeat to make three rows.

**Step 2.** Join the rows with seams pressed in alternating directions to complete a Nine-

Patch unit as shown in Figure 3. Repeat to complete 80 Nine-Patch units.

**Figure 3**

**Step 3.** To complete one 36-Patch Scrappy block, sew C and CR to B as shown in Figure 4; press seams toward C and CR. Repeat to make four B-C units.

**Figure 4**

**Step 4.** Sew a B-C unit to opposite sides of A as shown in Figure 5; press seams toward A.

**Figure 5**

**Step 5.** Sew a Nine-Patch unit to opposite sides of two B-C units referring to Figure 6; press seams toward the Nine-Patch units.

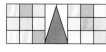

**Figure 6**

**Step 6.** Sew a B-C/Nine-Patch row to opposite sides of the A-B-C row to complete one 36-Patch Scrappy block; press seams toward the center row.

**Step 7.** Repeat Steps 3–6 to complete (20) 36-Patch Scrappy blocks, pressing seams in 10 blocks toward the center row and in the remaining 10 blocks away from the center row.

### Completing the Quilt

**Step 1.** Arrange and join four blocks to make a row; press seams in one direction. Repeat to complete five rows. ***Note:*** Join blocks in each row with seam allowances pressed in the same direction. Alternate the rows to allow for less bulk when sewing rows together.

**36-Patch Scrappy**
Placement Diagram 96" x 112"

**Step 2.** Join the rows to complete the pieced center; press seams in one direction.

**Step 3.** Join the E/F strips on short ends to make one long strip; press seams open. Subcut strip into two 80½" E strips and two 68½" F strips.

**Step 4.** Sew an E strip to opposite long sides and F strips to the top and bottom of the pieced center; press seams toward E and F strips.

**Step 5.** Join the G/H strips on short ends to make one long strip; press seams open. Subcut strip into two 84½" G strips and two 76½" H strips.

**Step 6.** Sew a G strip to opposite long sides and H strips to the top and bottom of the pieced center; press seams toward G and H strips.

**Step 7.** Select and join 46 D squares to create a long D strip; press seams in one direction. Repeat to make two long D strips.

**Step 8.** Repeat Step 5 with 40 D squares to make two short D strips.

**Step 9.** Sew a long D strip to each long side and short D strips to the top and bottom of the pieced center; press seams toward G and H strips.

**Step 10.** Join the I strips on short ends to make one long strip; press seams open. Subcut strip into four 96½" I strips.

**Step 11.** Sew an I strip to opposite long sides and to the top and bottom of the pieced center; press seams toward I strips.

**Step 12.** Finish the quilt referring to the Finishing Instructions on page 168. ◆

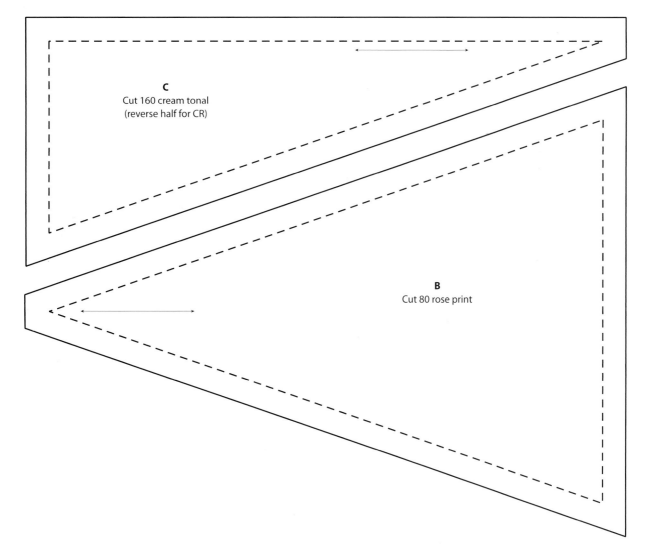

**C**
Cut 160 cream tonal
(reverse half for CR)

**B**
Cut 80 rose print

# Batik Scraps

Design by LUCY A. FAZELY & MICHAEL L. BURNS

## Use lots of batik scraps to make this beautiful bed-size quilt.

## Project Specifications

Skill Level: Beginner
Quilt Size: 80" x 96"
Pillowcase Size: 30½" x 20½"
Block Size: 16" x 16"
Number of Blocks: 30

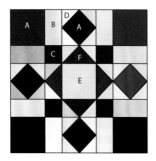

**Batik Light**
16" x 16" Block
Make 15

**Batik Dark**
16" x 16" Block
Make 15

| FABRIC<br>Measurements based on 42" usable fabric width. | #STRIPS & PIECES | CUT |
|---|---|---|
| Light batik scraps to total 5½ yards | 420 | 2½" D squares |
| | 135 | 4½" E squares |
| | 180 | 2½" x 4½" B rectangles |
| Dark batik scraps to total 5½ yards | 420 | 2½" C squares |
| | 135 | 4½" A squares |
| | 180 | 2½" x 4½" F rectangles |
| ¾ yard dark batik | 9 | 2¼" x 42" binding |
| Backing | | 86" x 102" |

### SUPPLIES

- Batting 86" x 102"
- Neutral color all-purpose thread
- Quilting thread
- Basic sewing tools and supplies

## Completing the Blocks

**Step 1.** Mark a diagonal line from corner to corner on the wrong side of 360 each C and D squares.

**Step 2.** Referring to Figure 1, place a C square on one end of B and stitch on the marked line; trim seam to ¼" and press C to the right side. Repeat with a second C on the remaining end of B to complete a B-C unit. Repeat to make 60 B-C units.

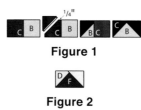

**Figure 1**

**Figure 2**

**Step 3.** Repeat step 2 with D and F to complete 60 D-F units as shown in Figure 2.

**Step 4.** Referring to Figure 3, place a C square on opposite corners of E; stitch on the marked lines, trim seam to ¼" and press C to the right side. Repeat on remaining corners of E to complete a C-E unit. Repeat to make 60 C-E units.

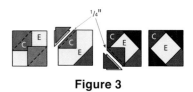

**Figure 3**

**Step 5.** Repeat step 4 with A and D to complete 60 A-D units as shown in Figure 4.

**Figure 4**

**Step 6.** Join one C-E unit with one B-C unit to make a dark side unit as shown in Figure 5; press seam toward C-E. Repeat to make 60 dark side units.

**Figure 5**

**Step 7.** Sew F to one side of E; sew D to one end of a second F; press seams toward F. Repeat to make 60 each E-F and F-D units.

**Step 8.** Join the E-F and D-F units to complete a dark corner unit as shown in Figure 6; press seam toward E-F. Repeat to make 60 dark corner units.

**Figure 6**

**Step 9.** To complete one Batik Dark block, sew a dark side unit to opposite sides of A to complete the dark center row as shown in Figure 7; press seams toward A.

**Figure 7**

**Step 10.** Sew a dark side unit between two dark corner units as shown in Figure 8 to complete the dark top row;

press seams toward the dark corner units. Repeat to make a dark bottom row.

**Figure 8**

**Step 11.** Sew the dark top and bottom rows to the dark center row referring to Figure 9 to complete one Batik Dark block; press seams away from the center row. Repeat to make 15 Batik Dark blocks.

**Figure 9**

**Step 12.** To complete one Batik Light block, refer to Figure 10 to complete 60 each light side and corner units.

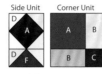

**Figure 10**

**Figure 11**

**Step 13.** Join the light units with an E square as shown in Figure 11 to make rows; join

the rows to complete one Batik Light block; press seams toward the center row. Repeat to make 15 Batik Light blocks.

## Completing the Quilt

**Step 1.** Join two Batik Dark and three Batik Light blocks to complete an X row; press seams toward the dark blocks. Repeat to make three X rows.

**Step 2.** Join two Batik Light and three Batik Dark blocks to complete a Y row; press seams toward the dark blocks. Repeat to make three Y rows.

**Step 3.** Join the X and Y rows to complete the pieced top; press seams in one direction.

**Step 4.** Layer, quilt and bind referring to Finishing Instructions on page 168. ◆

**Batik Scraps**
Placement Diagram
80" x 96"

# Dancing Colors

Design by CONNIE RAND

## Sort scraps into lights and darks and leave out the mediums before starting to stitch this really scrappy quilt.

### Project Specifications
Skill Level: Intermediate
Quilt Size: 70" x 86"
Block Size: 16" x 16"
Number of Blocks: 20

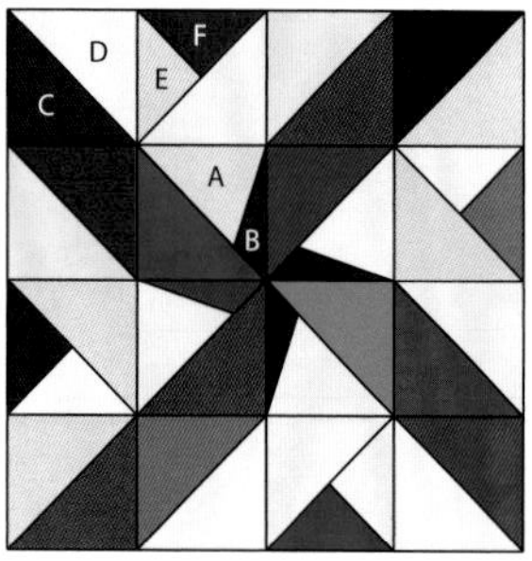

**Dancing Colors**
16" x 16" Block
Make 10

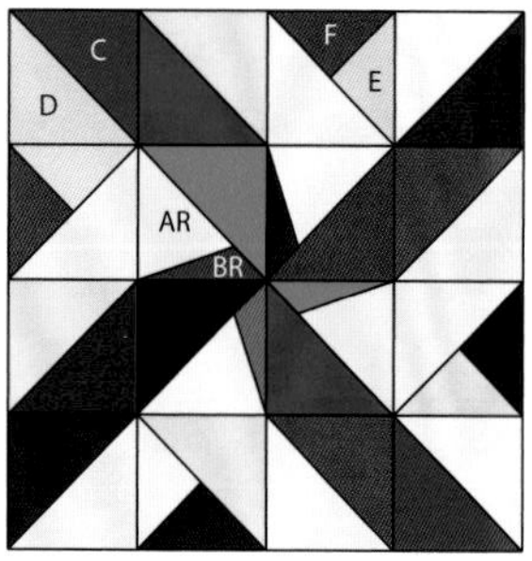

**Reversed Dancing Colors**
16" x 16" Block
Make 10

| FABRIC Measurements based on 42" usable fabric width. | #STRIPS & PIECES | CUT | #PIECES | SUBCUT |
|---|---|---|---|---|
| Assorted light scraps | | A pieces as directed on template | | |
| | 120 | 4⅞" squares | | Cut in half on 1 diagonal to make 240 D triangles |
| | 20 | 5¼" squares | | Cut on both diagonals to make 80 E triangles |
| Assorted dark scraps | | B pieces as directed on template | | |
| | 120 | 4⅞" squares | | Cut in half on 1 diagonal to make 240 C triangles |
| | 20 | 5¼" squares | | Cut on both diagonals to make 80 F triangles |
| 1½ yards blue mottled | 8 | 3½" x 42" G/H | | |
| | 8 | 2¼" x 42" binding | | |
| Backing | | 76" x 92" | | |

### SUPPLIES
- Batting 76" x 92"
- All-purpose thread to match fabrics
- Quilting thread
- Basic sewing tools and supplies

### Completing the Blocks
**Step 1.** Prepare templates for A and B pieces using patterns given; cut as directed on each piece.
**Step 2.** Join one each C and D triangles as shown in Figure 1;

press seam toward C. Repeat to make 160 C-D units.

Make 160

**Figure 1**

**Step 3.** Sew E to F and add D as shown in Figure 2; press seams toward F and D. Repeat to make 40 D-E-F units. Repeat to make 40 reverse D-E-F units, again referring to Figure 2.

Make 40 each
Reverse

**Figure 2**

**Step 4.** Sew A to B and AR to BR and add C referring to Figure 3; press seams toward B or BR and then C. Repeat to make 40 each A-B-C and reverse A-B-C units.

Make 40 each
Reverse

**Figure 3**

**Step 5.** Select eight C-D units and four each D-E-F and A-B-C units and arrange in rows to complete one Dancing Colors block as shown in Figure 4; press seams of adjacent rows in opposite directions. Repeat to make 10 Dancing Colors blocks. **Note:** *Try to use as many different fabrics as possible in each block.*

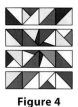

**Figure 4**

**Step 6.** Repeat Step 5 with eight C-D and four each reverse D-E-F and A-B-C units to complete 10 Reversed Dancing Colors blocks.

## Completing the Quilt

**Step 1.** Arrange two Dancing Colors blocks with two Reversed Dancing Colors blocks to make an X row as shown in Figure 5; press seams toward the Dancing Colors blocks. Repeat to make three X rows.

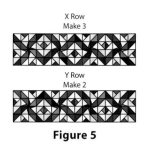

X Row
Make 3

Y Row
Make 2

**Figure 5**

**Step 2.** Arrange two Reversed Dancing Colors blocks with two Dancing Colors blocks to make a Y row, again referring to Figure 5; press seams toward the Dancing Colors blocks. Repeat to make two Y rows.

**Step 3.** Join the rows referring to the Placement Diagram to complete the pieced top; press seams in one direction.

**Step 4.** Join the G/H strips on short ends to make one long strip; press seams open. Subcut strip into two 80½" G strips and two 70½" H strips.

**Step 5.** Sew the G strips to opposite long sides and H strips to the top and bottom of the pieced center to complete the pieced top; press seams toward G and H strips.

**Step 6.** Finish the quilt referring to the Finishing Instructions on page 168 ◆

**Dancing Colors**
Placement Diagram 70" x 86"

## TIP

*Sometimes scrap quilts can get very busy looking. To simplify your pattern and the look of the quilt, chose two or three color families and gather only scraps of these colors to make your quilt.*

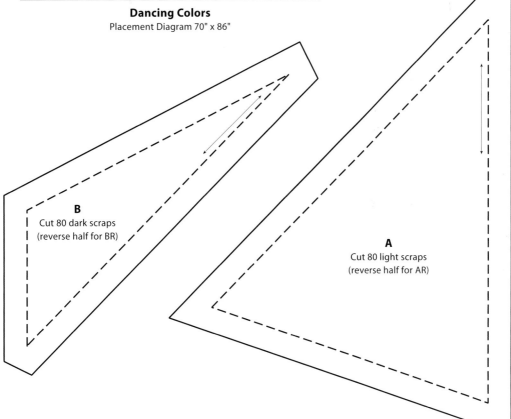

**B**
Cut 80 dark scraps
(reverse half for BR)

**A**
Cut 80 light scraps
(reverse half for AR)

# Twisted Spools

Design by LUCY A. FAZELY & MICHAEL L. BURNS

## Use a neutral background and light and dark fabrics in each block to make this scrappy-looking quilt.

### Project Specifications

Skill Level: Intermediate
Quilt Size: 82" x 92"
Block Size: 10" x 10"
Number of Blocks: 56

**Twisted Spool**
10" x 10" Block
Make 56

### Completing the Blocks

**Step 1.** Mark a diagonal line on the wrong side of each F and G square.

**Step 2.** Place an F square on the square corner of A as shown in Figure 1; stitch on the marked line, trim seam allowance to ¼" and press F open, again referring to Figure 1. Repeat with all F and G squares to make 56 each A-F and A-G units.

| FABRIC Measurements based on 42" usable fabric width. | #STRIPS & PIECES | CUT | #PIECES | SUBCUT |
|---|---|---|---|---|
| 14 assorted light fat quarters | 1 | 9⅛" square each | | Cut on both diagonals to make 56 C triangles total |
| | 4 | 2" x 9" E rectangles each | | |
| | 4 | 2" F squares each | | |
| 14 assorted dark fat quarters | 1 | 9⅛" square each | | Cut on both diagonals to make 56 B triangles total |
| | 4 | 2" x 9" D rectangles each | | |
| | 4 | 2" G squares each | | |
| ⅔ yard navy tonal | 8 | 2½" x 42" | | |
| 1¾ yards red tonal | 8 | 4½" x 42" | | |
| | 9 | 2¼" x 42" binding | | |
| 3½ yards white tonal | 10 | 11¼" x 42" | 28 | 11¼" squares; cut on both diagonals to make 112 A triangles |
| Backing | | 88" x 98" | | |

### SUPPLIES

- Batting 88" x 98"
- All-purpose thread to match fabrics
- Quilting thread
- Basting spray
- Basic sewing tools and supplies

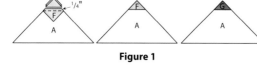

**Figure 1**

**Step 3.** Select one each same-color B and D pieces and A-G unit and one each same-color C and E pieces and A-F unit.

**Step 4.** To complete one Twisted Spool block, sew E to B and D to C matching one straight end as shown in Figure 2; press seams toward C and B.

**Figure 2**

**Step 5.** Trim the excess D and E even with B and C as shown in Figure 3.

**Figure 3**

**Step 6.** Sew the C-D unit to the A-F unit to complete half the block as shown in Figure 4; press seams toward A-F.

**Figure 4**

**Step 7.** Repeat Step 6 with A-G and B-E to complete the second half of the block, again referring to Figure 4.

**Step 8.** Join the two stitched halves to complete one block referring to the block drawing; press seam to one side.

**Step 9.** Repeat Steps 3–8 to complete 56 Twisted Spool blocks.

## Completing the Quilt

**Step 1.** Join seven blocks to complete an X row as shown in Figure 5; press seams toward vertical blocks. Make four X rows.

**Step 2.** Join seven blocks to complete a Y row, again referring to Figure 5; press seams toward vertical blocks. Make four Y rows.

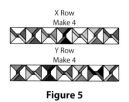

X Row
Make 4

Y Row
Make 4

**Figure 5**

**Step 3.** Join the rows, alternating rows and starting with an X row, to complete the pieced center; press seams in one direction.

**Step 4.** Join the H/I strips with right sides together on short ends to make one long strip; press seams open. Subcut strip into two 80½" H strips and two 74½" I strips.

**Step 5.** Sew H strips to opposite long sides and I strips to the top and bottom of the pieced center; press seams toward H and I strips.

**Step 6.** Join the J/K strips with right sides together on short ends to make one long strip; press seams open. Subcut strip into two 84½" J strips and two 82½" K strips.

**Step 7.** Sew J strips to opposite long sides and K strips to the top and bottom of the pieced center; press seams toward J and K strips.

**Step 8.** Finish the quilt referring to the Finishing Instructions on page 168. ◆

**Twisted Spools**
Placement Diagram 82" x 92"

# Cabins From Scraps

Design by PAT CAMPBELL

Paper-piecing these tiny Log Cabin blocks from scraps makes accurate results a cinch.

## Project Specifications

Skill Level: Intermediate
Quilt Size: 40" x 48"
Block Size: 4" x 4"
Number of Blocks: 88

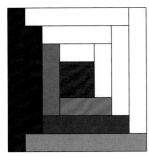

**Log Cabin**
4" x 4" Block
Make 88

## Completing the Blocks

**Step 1.** Set machine to a small stitch length to make removal of paper easier.

**Step 2.** Prepare copies of full-size paper-piecing pattern.

| FABRIC Measurements based on 42" usable fabric width. | #STRIPS & PIECES | CUT | #PIECES | SUBCUT |
|---|---|---|---|---|
| Assorted medium-to-dark scraps | 88 | 1½" #1 squares | | |
| | 45 | 1" x 42" | 88 | 2" #4 |
| | | | 88 | 2½" #5 |
| | | | 88 | 3" #8 |
| | | | 88 | 3½" #9 |
| | | | 88 | 4" #12 |
| | | | 88 | 4½" #13 |
| ½ yard dark print | 5 | 2¼" x 42" binding | | |
| 1¾ yards cream tonal | 4 | 4½" x 32½" A | | |
| | 39 | 1" x 42" | 88 | 1½" #2 |
| | | | 88 | 2" #3 |
| | | | 88 | 2½" #6 |
| | | | 88 | 3" #7 |
| | | | 88 | 3½" #10 |
| | | | 88 | 4" #11 |
| Backing | | 46" x 54" | | |

### SUPPLIES

- Batting 46" x 54"
- All-purpose thread to match fabrics
- Quilting thread
- Paper for patterns
- Basic sewing tools and supplies

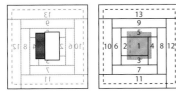

**Figure 1**

**Step 3.** To complete one Log Cabin block, place piece 1 right side up on the unmarked side of the paper, covering the piece 1 center section and extending ¼" into all surrounding sections.

Place piece 2 right sides together with piece 1 on the 1-2 seam side as shown in Figure 1; turn paper over and stitch on the marked 1-2 line.

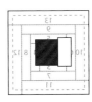

**Figure 2**

**Step 4.** Press piece 2 to the right side as shown in Figure 2.

**Step 5.** Continue adding pieces in numerical order in this manner until the entire paper foundation is covered.

**Step 6.** Trim finished foundation along outside-edge line if necessary to complete one block.

**Step 7.** Repeat Steps 3–6 to complete 88 Log Cabin blocks.

## Completing the Quilt

**Step 1.** Arrange and join 64 blocks in eight rows of eight blocks each referring to Figure 3; press seams in one direction.

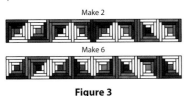

Make 2

Make 6

**Figure 3**

**Step 2.** Join the rows referring to the Placement Diagram for positioning; press seams in one direction.

**Step 3.** Sew an A strip to opposite sides of the pieced center; press seams toward A strips.

**Step 4.** Sew a Log Cabin block to each end of each remaining A strip as shown in Figure 4; press seams toward A strips.

A

**Figure 4**

**Step 5.** Sew an A/Log Cabin strip to the top and bottom of the pieced center; press seams toward the A/Log Cabin strips.

**Step 6.** Join 10 Log Cabin blocks as shown in Figure 5 to make the top strip; press seams in one direction. Repeat to make the bottom strip.

**Figure 5**

**Step 7.** Sew the top and bottom strips to the top and bottom of the pieced center referring to the Placement Diagram for positioning of strips to complete the pieced top.

**Step 8.** Remove paper foundations.

**Step 9.** Finish the quilt referring to the Finishing Instructions on page 168. ◆

**Cabins From Scraps**
Placement Diagram 40" x 48"

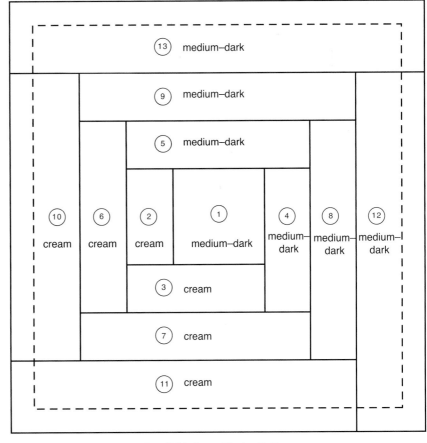

**Log Cabin Paper-Piecing Pattern**
Make 88 copies

# Leftovers Squared

Design by CONNIE RAND

If you have a stash of oddball scraps, you finally have an excuse to use them! Colors and prints don't matter as long as they're dark.

## Project Specifications

Skill Level: Intermediate
Quilt Size: 70" x 84"
Block Size: 14" x 14"
Number of Blocks: 30

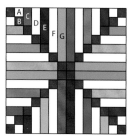

**Leftovers Squared**
14" x 14" Block
Make 30

| FABRIC Measurements based on 42" usable fabric width. | #STRIPS & PIECES | CUT | #PIECES | SUBCUT |
|---|---|---|---|---|
| 2 yards red solid | 32 | 1½" x 42" | 360 | 1½" B squares |
| | 8 | 2¼" x 42" binding | | |
| 3 yards white tonal | 9 | 1½" x 42" A | | |
| | 10 | 3½" x 42" | 120 | 1½" D rectangles |
| | 10 | 5½" x 42" | 120 | 1½" F rectangles |
| Assorted dark scraps | 240 | 1½" x 2½" C rectangles | | |
| | 240 | 1½" x 4½" E rectangles | | |
| | 240 | 1½" x 6½" G rectangles | | |
| Backing | | 76" x 90" | | |

### SUPPLIES

- Batting 76" x 90"
- All-purpose thread to match fabrics
- Quilting thread
- Basic sewing tools and supplies

## Completing the Blocks

**Step 1.** Sew an A strip to a B strip with right sides together along the length; press seams toward B. Repeat to make nine A-B strip sets.

**Step 2.** Subcut strip sets into (240) 1½" A-B units as shown in Figure 1.

**Figure 1**

**Step 3.** Sew a B strip to each D and F strip with right sides together along the length to make five each B-D and B-F strip sets; press seams away from B.

**Step 4.** Subcut strip sets into 120 each 1½" B-D and B-F segments as shown in Figure 2.

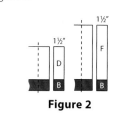

**Figure 2**

**Step 5.** To complete one Leftovers Squared block, join two A-B units to complete a Four-Patch unit as shown in Figure 3; press seam in one direction. Repeat to make four Four-Patch units.

**Figure 3**

**Step 6.** Sew a B square to four each C, E and G pieces referring to Figure 4; press seams away from B.

Make 4 each

**Figure 4**

**Step 7.** Referring to Figure 5, add a C rectangle to a Four-Patch unit; press seams toward C. Sew a B-C unit to one adjacent side; press seam toward B-C.

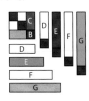

**Figure 5**

**Step 8.** Continue adding strips and units, again referring to Figure 5, to make one quarter of a Leftovers Squared block. Press seams toward most recently added piece as you stitch.

*TIP*
*As you cut pieces for other projects, cut 1½" strips from the leftovers and set them aside to make this quilt.*

**Step 9.** Repeat Steps 5–8 to complete four block quarters. Join quarters to complete the block as shown in Figure 6; press seams in one direction.

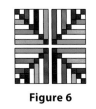

**Figure 6**

**Step 10.** Repeat Steps 5–9 to make 30 blocks.

### Completing the Quilt
**Step 1.** Arrange and join blocks in six rows of five blocks each as shown in Figure 7; press seams in alternate rows in opposite directions.

**Figure 7**

**Step 2.** Join rows to complete the top, referring to the Placement Diagram; press seams in one direction.

**Step 3.** Finish the quilt referring to the Finishing Instructions on page 168. ◆

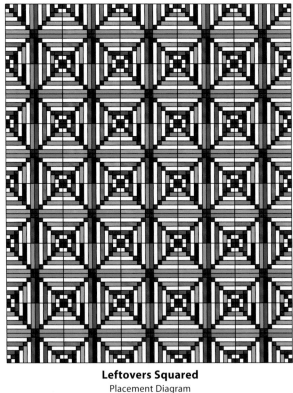

**Leftovers Squared**
Placement Diagram
70" x 84"

# Special Times Quilting

Although you can buy Christmas fabric with Christmas motifs, you can also use all your red and green scraps and create a delightful quilt that says, "Merry Christmas!" Likewise, take your collection of orange and black scraps to create a special Halloween quilt. Almost any quilt design can be turned into a holiday or seasonal quilt through the use of scraps in the colors of the occasion. Celebrate with a quilt!

# Holly Star Wreath

Design by BARBARA CLAYTON

## Candy-cane stripes combine with traditional holiday colors in this festive table quilt.

### Project Specifications
Skill Level: Intermediate
Quilt Size: 24" x 24"

### Making the Holly Berries
**Step 1.** To complete one berry, with a knotted length of thread to match berry fabric, hand-stitch a line of gathering stitches ⅛" from the edge all around each circle.

**Step 2.** With thread still in fabric, place a small amount of polyester fiberfill in the center of the berry; pull the thread tightly to gather around the fiberfill to form the berry as shown in Figure 1. Knot thread to hold.

**Figure 1**

**Step 3.** Repeat Steps 1 and 2 to complete 36 berries.

**Step 4.** Hand-stitch a cluster of three berries together with gathered openings on the back side; set aside.

### Preparing the Holly Leaves
**Step 1.** Trace leaf shapes onto the paper side of the freezer paper using the pattern given; layer and cut several layers

| FABRIC Measurements based on 42" usable fabric width. | #STRIPS & PIECES | CUT | #PIECES | SUBCUT |
|---|---|---|---|---|
| Light and medium green scraps for leaves | | Leaves as directed on pattern | | |
| Dark green scraps | | E as directed on template | | |
| ⅛ yard red solid | | Berries as directed on pattern | | |
| ¼ yard medium green print | | E as directed on template | | |
| ¼ yard red-and-white stripe | | D as directed on template | | |
| ¼ yard medium green mottled | 4 | 2½" x 20½" H | | |
| ½ yard red mottled | 1 | 4½" A square | | |
| | 1 | 3½" x 42" | 8 | 3½" C squares |
| | 3 | 2¼" x 42" binding | | |
| ½ yard white-with-black dots | | B as directed on template | | |
| | 1 | 3½" x 42" | 8 | 3½" F squares |
| | | | 4 | 2½" I squares |
| | 2 | 5¼" squares | | Cut on both diagonals to make 8 G triangles |
| Backing | | 30" x 30" | | |

### SUPPLIES
- Batting 30" x 30"
- Polyester fiberfill
- All-purpose thread to match fabrics
- Quilting thread
- Clear nylon thread
- Fabric glue stick
- Freezer paper
- Sponge or cloth
- Basic sewing tools and supplies

at a time to cut 24 freezer-paper leaves.

**Step 2.** Press the waxy side of the freezer paper onto the

wrong side of fabrics as directed on pattern for color.

**Step 3.** Cut out leaf shapes leaving a ¼" seam allowance beyond the freezer-paper edges.

*TIP*

*Test the red fabrics to be sure they are colorfast before using. If they are not, do not use a marking pen that has to be moistened when removed because the red will bleed into the lighter fabrics.*

*Be careful when wetting to remove freezer paper from behind leaf shapes to avoid color bleeding.*

**Step 4.** Clip leaf points and indentations almost to the paper pattern.

**Step 5.** Using a fabric glue stick, glue the ¼" excess fabric over the edge and to the back of the freezer paper; glue all the way around each piece. Set aside to appliqué later.

### Completing the Quilt

**Step 1.** Mark dots given on templates onto fabric pieces.

**Step 2.** Pin B to BR on the short sides and stitch from dot to dot, locking stitches at the beginning and end of seam as shown in Figure 2; press seam open. Repeat to make four B-BR units.

**Figure 2**

**Step 3.** Set a D square in between the B-BR points to complete a B-D unit as shown in Figure 3, stitching from dot to dot and locking stitches at the beginning and end; press

seams toward B and BR. Repeat to complete four B-D units.

**Figure 3**

**Step 4.** Sew a B-D unit to opposite sides of A to make an A-B-D unit as shown in Figure 4; press seams away from A.

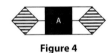

**Figure 4**

**Step 5.** Sew a C square to each end of each remaining B-D unit to make a B-D-C unit as shown in Figure 5; press seams toward C. Repeat to make two B-D-C units.

**Figure 5**

**Step 6.** Sew a B-D-C unit to opposite sides of the A-B-D unit to complete the center unit as shown in Figure 6.

**Figure 6**

**Step 7.** Sew a dark green mottled E piece to each side of a green print E piece to make an E unit as shown in Figure 7; press seams open. Repeat to make eight E units.

**Figure 7**

**Step 8.** Set an E unit between the points of the D and C squares as shown in Figure 8; press seams open. Repeat around the center unit.

**Figure 8**

**Step 9.** Join the seams between the E units to complete the star design; press seams to one side.

**Step 10.** Set in G triangles and F squares with C squares in the corners as shown in Figure 9 to complete the piecing.

**Figure 9**

**Step 11.** Arrange two holly leaves approximately ¼" from each corner of A with the first two spikes of each leaf over the seam as shown in Figure 10; when satisfied with placement, machine zigzag-stitch in place using clear nylon thread.

**Figure 10**

**Step 12.** Arrange two holly leaves on each F square and stitch in place as in Step 11, overlapping leaves as shown in Figure 11.

**Figure 11**

**Step 13.** Sew an H strip to opposite sides of the pieced center; press seams toward H strips.

**Step 14.** Sew an I square to each end of each remaining H strip; press seams toward H strips. Sew an H-I strip to the remaining sides of the pieced center.

**Step 15.** From the wrong side, make a slit behind each of the 24 leaf shapes; cut away the backing to within ¼" of the appliqué stitching. Use a sponge or a cloth to wet the back of the appliqué; tear away the freezer paper from behind each leaf. Let dry and lightly press.

**Step 16.** Finish the quilt referring to the Finishing Instructions on page 168.

**Step 17.** Sew a berry cluster over the ends of the leaves on A and F to complete the quilt. ◆

**Holly Star Wreath**
Placement Diagram 24" x 24"

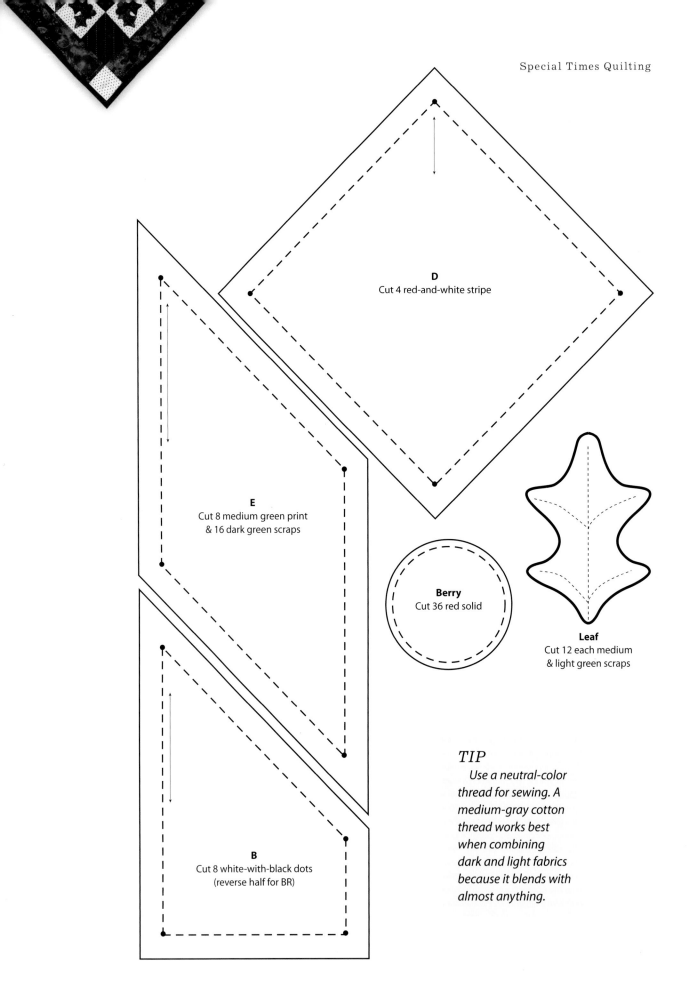

**D**
Cut 4 red-and-white stripe

**E**
Cut 8 medium green print
& 16 dark green scraps

**Berry**
Cut 36 red solid

**Leaf**
Cut 12 each medium
& light green scraps

**B**
Cut 8 white-with-black dots
(reverse half for BR)

*TIP*

*Use a neutral-color thread for sewing. A medium-gray cotton thread works best when combining dark and light fabrics because it blends with almost anything.*

# Really Scrappy Log Cabin

Design by SANDRA L. HATCH

Cut lots of holiday scraps into 2"-wide strips and join to make long strips for this simple Log Cabin quilt.

## Project Specifications

Skill Level: Beginner
Quilt Size: 72" x 90"
Block Size: 15" x 15"
Number of Blocks: 12

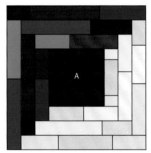

**Log Cabin**
15" x 15" Block
Make 12

| FABRIC<br>Measurements based on 42" usable fabric width. | #STRIPS & PIECES | CUT | #PIECES | SUBCUT |
|---|---|---|---|---|
| 1100" of 2"-wide strips light holiday prints | | Cut as per instructions for D and E | | |
| 900" of 2"-wide strips dark holiday prints | | Cut as per instructions for D and E | | |
| 12—6½" poinsettia A squares | | | | |
| ⅓ yard white holiday print | 2 | 3½" x 42" | 20 | 3½" C squares |
| ⅔ yard red print | 8 | 2¼" x 42" binding | | |
| 3⅝ yards black holiday print | 3 | 15½" x 42" | 31 | 3½" B pieces |
| | 2 | 6½" x 78½" F along length | | |
| | 2 | 6½" x 72½" G along length | | |
| Backing | | 78" x 96" | | |

## SUPPLIES

- Batting 78" x 96"
- All-purpose thread to match fabrics
- Quilting thread
- Basic sewing tools and supplies

## Completing the Blocks

**Step 1.** Join the light strips in random order with right sides together on short ends to make multiple long strips; press seams in one direction. **Note:** *The length of the strips doesn't matter; making three or four long strips from the scraps rather than just one long strip makes them easier to work with when sewing.*

**Step 2.** Repeat Step 1 with the dark strips.

**Figure 1**

**Step 3.** Place an A square right sides together with a light strip and stitch as shown in Figure 1; continue adding A squares to the strip until you have finished with all 12 A squares.

**Step 4.** Lay the stitched strip flat on a surface with the A squares on the top and the strip

on the bottom as shown in Figure 2.

**Figure 2**

**Step 5.** Using a rotary cutter and straightedge, trim the strip even with the edge of the block as shown in Figure 3; repeat on each block. Press seams toward the strips.

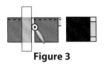

**Figure 3**

**Step 6.** Place the blocks with strip edges facing you on the light strip and sew as in Step 3 as shown in Figure 4; trim and press as in Steps 4 and 5.

**Figure 4**

**Step 7.** Continue with the next two sides using a dark strip to complete one round of strips as shown in Figure 5.

**Figure 5**

**Step 8.** Continue adding strips around the center in numerical order referring to Figure 6 to complete 12 Log Cabin blocks.

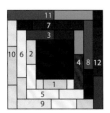

**Figure 6**

**Step 9.** Square-up blocks to 15½" x 15½" if necessary.

## Completing the Quilt

**Step 1.** Join three Log Cabin blocks with four B sashing strips to make a block row as shown in Figure 7; press seams toward B strips. Repeat to make four block rows.

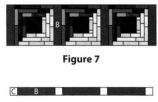

**Figure 7**

**Figure 8**

**Step 2.** Join four C squares with three B sashing strips to make a sashing row referring to Figure 8; press seams toward B strips. Repeat to make five sashing rows.

**Step 3.** Join the block rows and sashing rows to complete the pieced center; press seams toward sashing rows.

**Step 4.** Cut two 75½" D strips and two 60½" E strips from the joined light strips.

**Step 5.** Sew D strips to opposite long sides and E strips to the top and bottom of the pieced center; press seams toward D and E strips.

**Step 6.** Sew F strips to opposite long sides and G strips to the top and bottom of the pieced center to complete the pieced top; press seams toward F and G strips.

**Step 7.** Finish the quilt referring to the Finishing Instructions on page 168. ◆

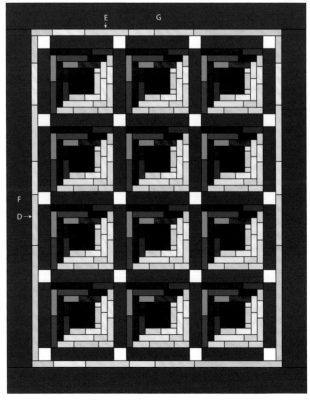

**Really Scrappy Log Cabin**
Placement Diagram 72" x 90"

# Shiny Ornaments

Design by CATE TALLMAN-EVANS

## Metallic prints add the sparkle to this pretty holiday quilt. It's easy enough for a beginner to make.

### Project Specifications
Skill Level: Beginner
Quilt Size: 66" x 79"
Block Size: 12" x 12"
Number of Blocks: 20

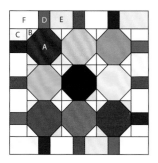

**Ornaments**
12" x 12" Block
Make 20

| FABRIC Measurements based on 42" usable fabric width. | #STRIPS & PIECES | CUT | #PIECES | SUBCUT |
|---|---|---|---|---|
| ½ yard each 4 red and 5 gold metallic prints | 2 | 3½" x 42" each | 20 | 3½" A squares each—180 total |
| | | | 12 | 1½" H squares total |
| | 8 | 2¼" x 42" binding | | |
| ⅝ yard each 4 cream metallic prints | 26 | 1½" x 42" total | 720 | 1½" B squares |
| | 4 | 1½" x 42" C total | | |
| | 8 | 2½" x 42" E total | | |
| | 4 | 3" x 42" F total | | |
| ⅝ yard each 3 green metallic prints | 12 | 1½" x 42" D total | | |
| | 11 | 1½" x 42" total | 31 | 12½" G strips |
| | 7 | 2" x 42" total | 2 | 12½" I strips |
| | | | 10 | 13½" J strips |
| | | | 2 | 14½" K strips |
| | | | 4 | 14" L strips |
| 1⅜ yards red-and-green metallic print | 7 | 6½" x 42" M/N | | |
| Backing | | 72" x 85" | | |

### SUPPLIES

- Batting 72" x 85"
- All-purpose thread to match fabrics
- Quilting thread
- Basic sewing tools and supplies

### Completing the Blocks
**Step 1.** Mark a diagonal line from corner to corner on the wrong side of each B square.
**Step 2.** Place a B square right sides together on each corner of an A square and stitch on the marked line as shown in Figure 1. Trim seam to ¼"; press seam toward B to complete one A-B unit. Repeat with all A and B squares to complete 180 A-B units.

**Figure 1**

**Step 3.** Join two each C and E strips with three D strips with right sides together along length to make a C-D-E strip set referring to Figure 2; press seams toward D. Repeat to make two C-D-E strip sets.
**Step 4.** Subcut the C-D-E strip sets into (40) 2" C-D-E units, again referring to Figure 2.

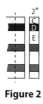

**Figure 2**

**Step 5.** Join two each E and F strips and three D strips with right sides together along

length to make a D-E-F strip set referring to Figure 3; press seams toward D. Repeat to make two D-E-F strip sets.

**Step 6.** Subcut the D-E-F strip sets into (40) 2" D-E-F units, again referring to Figure 3.

**Figure 3**

**Step 7.** To complete one Ornaments block, select nine A-B units. Join three A-B units to make a row as shown in Figure 4; press seams in one direction. ***Note:*** *In the sample shown, the A-B units are in the same position*

*in each block. Repeat to make three rows.*

**Figure 4**

**Step 8.** Join the rows to complete the block center referring to Figure 5; press seams in one direction.

**Figure 5**

**Step 9.** Sew a C-D-E unit to opposite sides and a D-E-F unit to the remaining sides to complete one Ornaments block; press seams away from the block center.

**Step 10.** Repeat Steps 7–9 to complete 20 Ornaments blocks.

## Completing the Quilt

**Step 1.** Join four Ornaments blocks with three G strips to make a block row as shown in Figure 6; press seams toward G strips. Repeat to make five block rows.

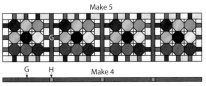

**Figure 6**

**Step 2.** Join four G strips with three H squares to make a sashing row, again referring to Figure 6; press seams toward G strips. Repeat to make four sashing rows.

**Step 3.** Join the block rows with the sashing rows to complete the pieced center; press seams toward sashing rows.

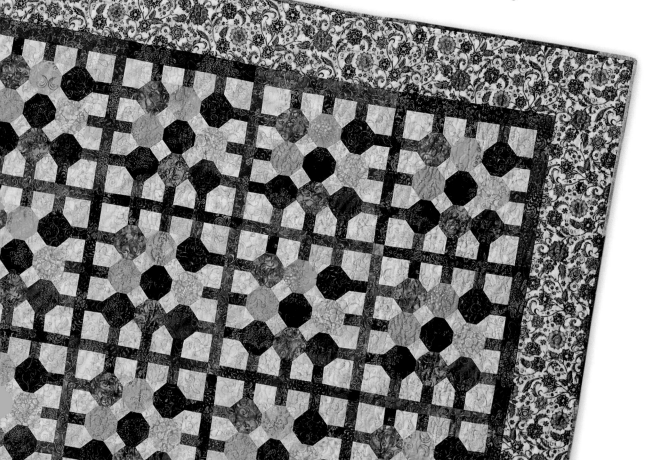

**Step 4.** Join four J strips with one I strip to make a side row referring to Figure 7; press seams in one direction. Repeat to make two side rows.

**Step 5.** Sew a side row to opposite long sides of the pieced center; press seams toward the side rows.

**Step 6.** Join two L strips with one each J and K strips to make the top row, again referring to Figure 7; press seams in one direction. Repeat to make the bottom row.

*TIP*

*If you find some of your scraps seem to stand out from the rest, try to place them in different areas of the quilt rather than all in one area.*

**Step 7.** Sew the top and bottom rows to the pieced center; press seams toward the top and bottom rows.

**Step 8.** Join the M/N strips with right sides together on short ends to make one long strip; press seams open.

Subcut strip into two 67½" M strips and two 66½" N strips.

**Step 9.** Sew the M strips to opposite long sides and N strips to the top and bottom of the pieced center; press seams toward M and N strips to complete the pieced top.

**Step 10.** Finish the quilt referring to the Finishing Instructions on page 168. ◆

Make 2

J · · · I

Make 2

L · K · J

**Figure 7**

**Shiny Ornaments Quilt**
Placement Diagram 66" x 79"

# Pumpkin Patch Visitors

Design by CHRISTINE SCHULTZ

## Whether made in planned colors or scraps, this quilt is the perfect harvest decoration.

### Project Specifications

Skill Level: Intermediate
Quilt Size: 46¾" x 46¾"
Block Size: 12" x 12"
Number of Blocks: 5

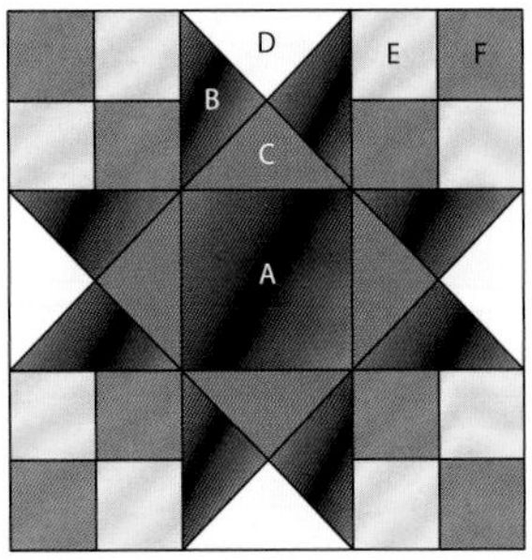

**Four-Patch Star**
12" x 12" Block
Make 5

### Project Note

To reduce the amount of seams under the appliqué, rectangles of the cream/tan print have been used in place of two or more squares in the sample quilt whenever possible.

### Completing the Blocks

**Step 1.** Sew an E strip to an F strip with right sides together along length to make an E-F strip set; press seam toward F. Repeat to make three strip sets.
**Step 2.** Subcut E-F strip sets into (40) 2½" E-F segments as shown in Figure 1.

| FABRIC Measurements based on 42" usable fabric width. | #STRIPS & PIECES | CUT | #PIECES | SUBCUT |
|---|---|---|---|---|
| Gray scrap | | Appliqué pieces as per pattern | | |
| Brown scrap | | Appliqué pieces as per pattern | | |
| Green scraps | | Appliqué pieces as per pattern | | |
| | 4 | 1" x 16" bias strips for vines | | |
| ¼ yard black print | | Appliqué pieces as per pattern | | |
| ¼ yard green print | 1 | 5¼" x 42" | 5 | 5¼" squares; cut on both diagonals to make 20 C triangles |
| ⅓ yard peach mottled | 3 | 2½" x 42" E | | |
| ⅓ yard orange print | | Appliqué pieces as per pattern | | |
| ½ yard salmon print | 3 | 2½" x 42" F | | |
| | 1 | 4½" x 42" | 4 | 4½" H squares |
| 1⅓ yards cream/tan print | 1 | 5¼" x 42" | 5 | 5¼" squares; cut on both diagonals to make 20 D triangles |
| | 3 | 4½" x 42" | 4 | 12½" J rectangles |
| | | | 4 | 8½" I rectangles |
| | | | 4 | 4½" G squares |
| | 1 | 12⅝" x 42" | 2 | 12⅝" squares; cut on both diagonals to make 4 L triangles |
| | 1 | 9⅜" x 42" | 2 | 9⅜" squares; cut in half on 1 diagonal to make 4 K triangles |

| FABRIC<br>Measurements based on 42" usable fabric width. | #STRIPS & PIECES | CUT | #PIECES | SUBCUT |
|---|---|---|---|---|
| 1½ yards black/ multicolored print | 1<br>2 | 4½" x 42"<br>5¼" x 42" | 5<br>10 | 4½" A squares<br>5¼" squares; cut on both diagonals to make 40 B triangles |
| | 2<br>3<br>5 | 4" x 40¼" M<br>4" x 42" N<br>2¼" x 42" binding | | |
| Backing | | 53" x 53" | | |

## SUPPLIES

- Batting 53" x 53"
- All-purpose thread to match fabrics
- Quilting thread
- Black embroidery floss
- ¼" bias-strip maker
- Freezer paper
- Basic sewing tools and supplies

**Figure 1**

**Step 3.** Join two E-F segments to make a Four-Patch unit as shown in Figure 2; press seam in one direction. Repeat to make 20 Four-Patch units.

**Figure 2**

**Step 4.** Join two B and one each C and D triangles to make a side unit as shown in Figure 3; press seams toward B. Repeat to make 20 side units.

**Figure 3**

**Step 5.** To complete one Four-Patch Star block, sew a side unit to opposite sides of A to make the center row as shown in Figure 4; press seams toward A.

**Figure 4**

**Step 6.** Sew a Four-Patch unit to opposite sides of a side unit to make a side row as shown in Figure 5; press seams toward the Four-Patch units. Repeat to make two side rows.

**Figure 5**

**Step 7.** Sew a side row to opposite sides of the center row to complete one Four-Patch Star block; press seams toward the center row.

**Step 8.** Repeat Steps 5–7 to complete five Four-Patch Star blocks.

## Completing the Quilt

**Step 1.** Sew an H square to a G square and add an I rectangle to make a G-H-I unit as shown in Figure 6; press seams toward H

and then I. Repeat to make four G-H-I units.

**Figure 6**

**Step 2.** Sew an L triangle to two adjacent sides of a G-H-I unit to complete an L side unit as shown in Figure 7; press seams toward L. Repeat to make four L side units.

**Figure 7**

**Step 3.** Join three Four-Patch Star blocks with two J rectangles and two K triangles to complete the center row as shown in Figure 8; press seams toward J and K.

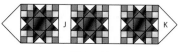

**Figure 8**

**Step 4.** Join two L side units with one Four-Patch Star block and one each J rectangle and K triangle to make a corner unit as shown in Figure 9; press seams away from the block. Repeat to make two corner units.

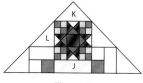

**Figure 9**

**Step 5.** Sew a corner unit to opposite sides of the center row to complete the pieced top; press seams away from the center row.

**Step 6.** Join the N strips on short ends to make one long

strip; press seams open. Subcut strip into two 47¼" N strips.

**Step 7.** Sew the M strips to opposite sides and N strips to the top and bottom of the pieced center; press seams toward M and N strips.

### Completing the Appliqué

**Step 1.** Press the edges of the vine bias strips over the ¼" bias-strip maker to make ¼" x 16" bias strips for vines; trim ends square.

**Step 2.** Cut four 7" x 9" rectangles freezer paper. Fold one rectangle in half with paper side out to make a 7" x 4½" rectangle.

**Step 3.** Open the paper and align the creased line with the center of the pumpkin pattern; trace half the pumpkin on the dull side on one side of the creased line. Refold paper and trace drawn line onto the other side of the creased line using a light table or sunny window.

**Step 4.** Unfold paper and staple four rectangles of paper together with the traced pattern on top. Cut out all four pumpkin shapes on the traced line and remove staples.

**Step 5.** Using patterns given, trace crows, leaves and beaks on the dull side of the freezer paper as directed on each piece; cut out shapes on drawn lines.

**Step 6.** Choose appliqué fabrics and iron the freezer-paper patterns to the wrong side as directed on patterns for color. Cut out shapes, adding about a ³⁄₁₆" turn-under seam allowance beyond the edge of the paper.

**Step 7.** Turn under edges of fabric and press over freezer paper; remove paper.

**Figure 10**

**Step 8.** Referring to Figure 10 and the Placement Diagram for positioning, pin and hand- or machine-stitch pieces in place in

### TIP

*Spray the bias strips lightly with spray starch before pressing over the bias bar to help create a crisp folded edge.*

this order: vines, stems, pumpkins, crows, beaks and leaves.

**Step 9.** Transfer lines for crows' feet onto the quilt top; stem-stitch using 3 strands black embroidery floss to complete the pieced top.

**Step 10.** Finish the quilt referring to the Finishing Instructions on page 168. ***Note:*** *The quilting design given may be used in the K and L triangles and the M and N borders.* ◆

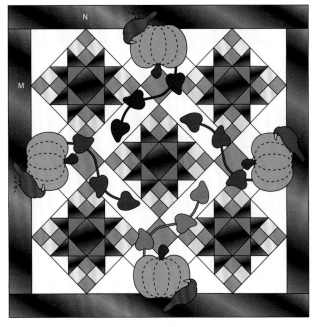

**Pumpkin Patch Visitors**
Placement Diagram 46³⁄₄" x 46³⁄₄"

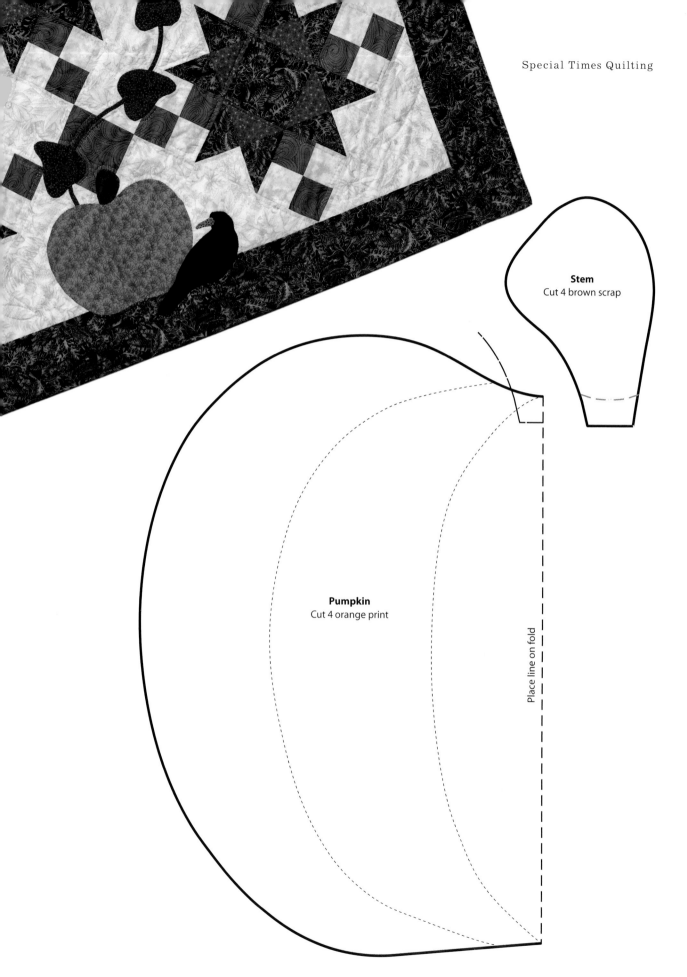

**Stem**
Cut 4 brown scrap

**Pumpkin**
Cut 4 orange print

Place line on fold

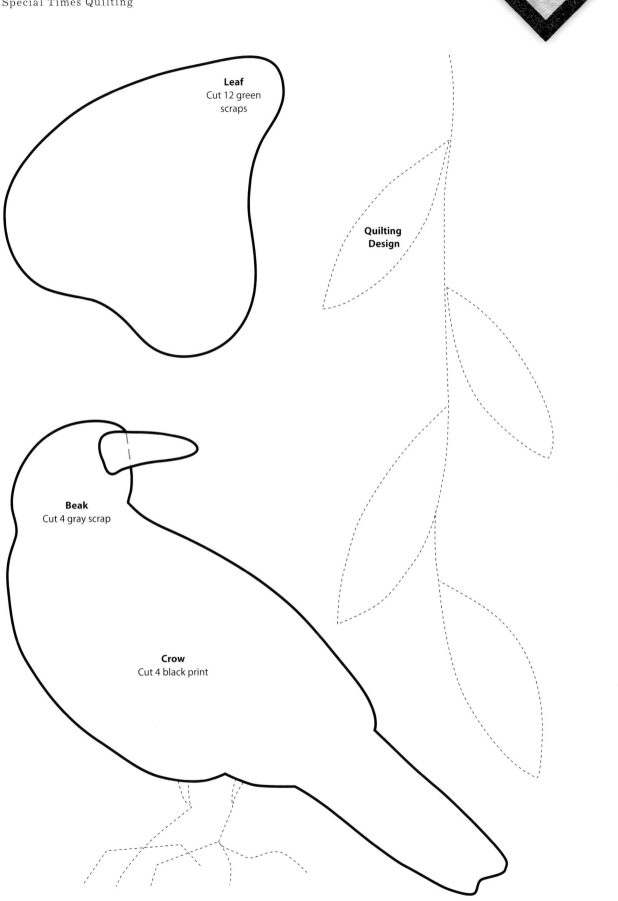

**Leaf**
Cut 12 green
scraps

**Quilting
Design**

**Beak**
Cut 4 gray scrap

**Crow**
Cut 4 black print

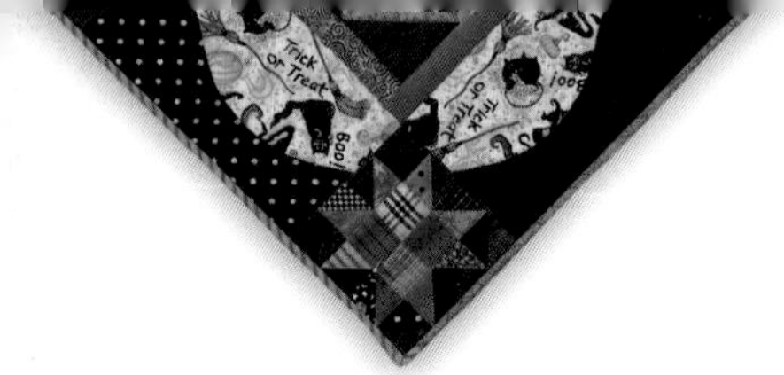



# It's Halloween Time

Design by JODI WARNER

Dig out those Halloween scraps and add some accent colors to make this simple Halloween quilt.

### Project Specifications

Skill Level: Beginner
Quilt Size: 47¾" x 47¾"
Block Size: 6¾" x 6¾" and 6" x 6"
Number of Blocks: 25 and 4

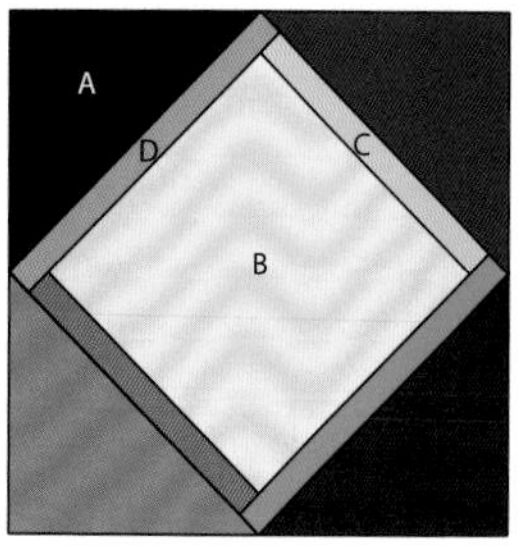


**Framed Square**
6³/₄" x 6³/₄" Block
Make 13

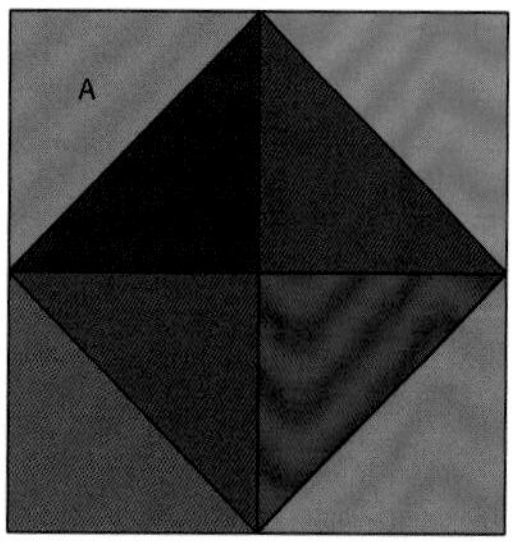


**Triangles-in-a-Square**
6³/₄" x 6³/₄" Block
Make 12

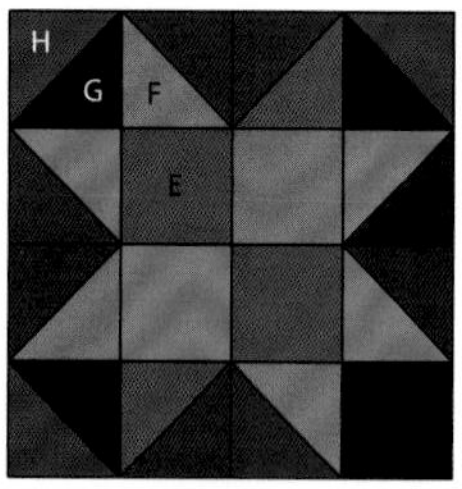


**Corner Block**
6" x 6" Block
Make 4

| **FABRIC** Measurements based on 42" usable fabric width. | #STRIPS & PIECES | CUT | #PIECES | SUBCUT |
|---|---|---|---|---|
| Black, orange and purple scraps | 74 | 4¼" A squares total | | Cut 26 squares in half on 1 diagonal to make 52 A triangles |
| | 16 | 2" orange E squares | | |
| | 16 | 2⅜" orange F squares | | |
| | 24 | 2⅜" black G squares | | |
| | 8 | 2⅜" purple H squares | | |
| | | 2¼" orange strips to total 220" for binding | | |
| | | K and L pieces as per patterns | | |
| 1⅛ yards Halloween print | 2 | 4½" x 42" | 13 | 4½" B squares |
| | 4 | 6½" x 36¼" M | | |
| Backing | | 54" x 54" | | |

**SUPPLIES**

- Batting 54" x 54"
- All-purpose thread to match fabrics
- Quilting thread
- Basic sewing tools and supplies

### Completing the Corner Blocks

**Step 1.** Draw a diagonal line from corner to corner on all F and H squares.

**Step 2.** Place an F square right sides together with a G square; stitch ¼" on each side of the marked line as shown in Figure 1; cut apart on the drawn line and press seam toward G to complete two F-G units. Repeat to complete 32 units.

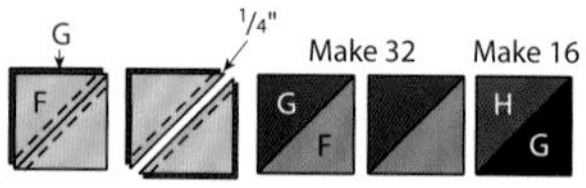


**Figure 1**

**Step 3.** Repeat Step 2 with G and H squares to make 16 G-H units, again referring to Figure 1.

**Step 4.** To complete one Corner Block, join two E squares; press seam in one direction. Repeat to make two E units.

**Step 5.** Join the two E units to complete the block center; press seam in one direction.

**Step 6.** Join two F-G units to make a side unit as shown in Figure 2; press seam in one direction. Repeat to make four side units.

**Figure 2**

**Step 7.** Sew a side unit to opposite sides of the center unit to complete the center row as shown in Figure 3; press seams toward the center unit.

**Figure 3**

**Step 8.** Sew a G-H unit to each end of each remaining side unit to complete the top and bottom rows as shown in Figure 4; press seams toward G-H.

**Figure 4**

**Step 9.** Sew the top and bottom rows to the center row to complete one Corner Block referring to the block drawing.

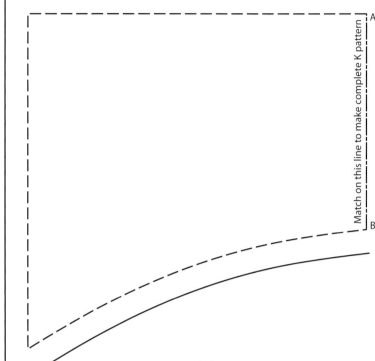

Match on this line to make complete K pattern

A

B

**Step 10.** Repeat Steps 4–9 to complete four Corner Blocks.

## Completing the Triangles-in-a-Square Blocks

**Step 1.** Draw a diagonal line from corner to corner on the wrong side of 24 A squares.

**Step 2.** Pair a marked square with an unmarked square with right sides together; stitch ¼" on each side of the marked line, again referring to Figure 5.

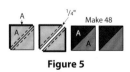

**Figure 5**

**Step 3.** Cut apart on the drawn line and press seams in one direction to make two A units.

**Step 4.** Repeat Steps 2 and 3

with the remaining A squares to make 48 A units.

**Step 5.** To complete one Triangles-in-a-Square block, join two A units to make an A row; press seam in one direction. Repeat to make two A rows.

**Step 6.** Join the two A rows referring to the block drawing to complete one block; press.

**Step 7.** Repeat Steps 5 and 6 to complete 12 Triangles-in-a-Square blocks.

## Completing the Framed Square Blocks

**Step 1.** To complete one Framed Square block, sew C to opposite sides of B; press seams toward C. Repeat with D on remaining sides of B; press seams toward D.

**Step 2.** Sew an A triangle to each side of the B-C-D unit referring to the block drawing to complete one block; press seams toward A.

**K**
Cut 8 black scraps
(reverse 4 for KR)

**Step 3.** Repeat Steps 1 and 2 to complete 13 Framed Square blocks.

## Completing the Quilt

**Step 1.** Join two Triangles-in-a-Square blocks with three Framed Square blocks to make an X row as shown in Figure 6; press seams toward the Framed Square blocks. Repeat to make three X rows.

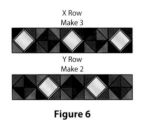

X Row
Make 3

Y Row
Make 2

**Figure 6**

**Step 2.** Join two Framed Square blocks with three Triangles-in-a-Square blocks to make a Y row, again referring to Figure 6; press seams toward the Framed Square blocks. Repeat to make two Y rows.

**Step 3.** Join the X and Y rows referring to the Placement

Diagram to complete the pieced center; press seams in one direction.

**Step 4.** Sew an I strip to opposite sides and a J strip to the top and bottom of the pieced center; press seams toward I and J strips.

**Step 5.** Prepare templates for K and L using patterns given. Cut as directed on each piece.

**Step 6.** Sew K and KR to L to make one K-L border unit as shown in Figure 7; press seams toward L. Repeat to make four units.

**Figure 7**

**Step 7.** Turn the curved edge under ¼"; press.

**Step 8.** Place a K-L unit on an M strip with straight edges aligned; pin to hold.

**Step 9.** Hand- or machine-appliqué the curved edge in

place using black thread. Trim away the M strip under the K-L unit, leaving a ¼" seam allowance.

**Step 10.** Repeat Steps 8 and 9 to complete four K-L-M units.

**Step 11.** Sew a K-L-M unit to opposite sides of the pieced center referring to the Placement Diagram for positioning of units; press seams toward the K-L-M units.

**Step 12.** Sew a Corner Block to each end of each remaining K-L-M unit; press seams away from the corner blocks. Sew these strips to the remaining sides of the pieced center; press seams toward the strips to complete the pieced top.

**Step 13.** Finish the quilt referring to the Finishing Instructions on page 168. ◆

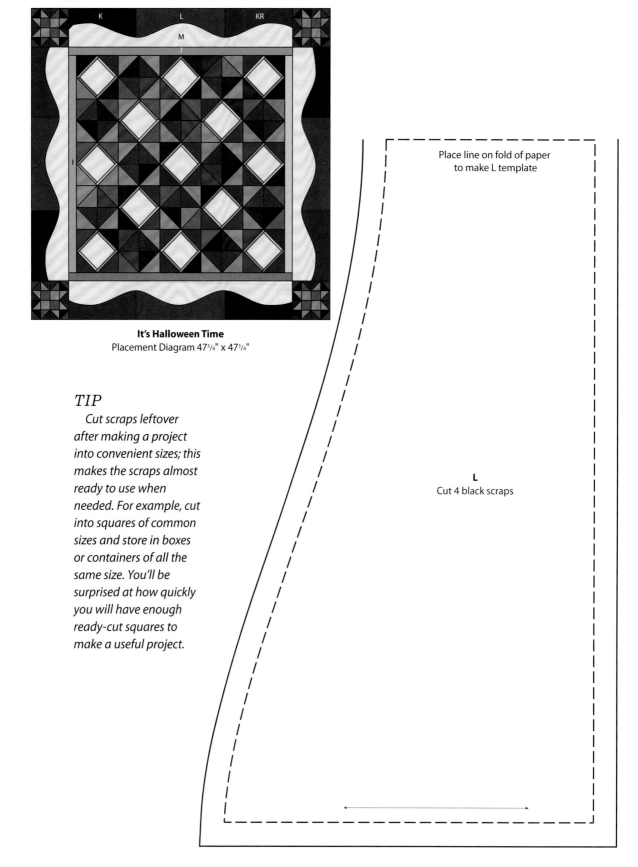

**It's Halloween Time**
Placement Diagram 47³/₄" x 47³/₄"

*TIP*

Cut scraps leftover after making a project into convenient sizes; this makes the scraps almost ready to use when needed. For example, cut into squares of common sizes and store in boxes or containers of all the same size. You'll be surprised at how quickly you will have enough ready-cut squares to make a useful project.

Place line on fold of paper
to make L template

**L**
Cut 4 black scraps

# Halloween Spider Web

Design by JULIA DUNN

Trade Halloween scraps with local or Internet friends to gather up enough to make a spooky quilt for trick or treat.

## Project Specifications
Skill Level: Beginner
Quilt Size: 53" x 58"
Block Size: 5" x 5"
Number of Blocks: 90

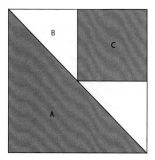

**Spider Web**
5" x 5" Block
Make 90

| FABRIC Measurements based on 42" usable fabric width. | #STRIPS & PIECES | CUT | #PIECES | SUBCUT |
|---|---|---|---|---|
| Halloween scraps | 45 | 5⅞" squares | | Cut in half on 1 diagonal to make 90 A triangles |
| | 90 | 3" C squares | | |
| Cream scraps | 90 | 3⅜" squares | | Cut in half on 1 diagonal to make 180 B triangles |
| 1⅝ yards black stripe | 2 | 4½" x 50½" D along length | | |
| | 2 | 4½" x 53½" E along length | | |
| | 5 | 2¼" binding along length | | |
| Backing | | 59" x 64" | | |

### SUPPLIES
- Batting 59" x 64"
- All-purpose thread to match fabrics
- Quilting thread
- Basic sewing tools and supplies

## Completing the Blocks
**Step 1.** To complete one Spider Web block, sew B to two adjacent sides of C as shown in Figure 1; press seams toward C.
**Step 2.** Sew the B-C unit to A to complete one Spider Web block.

**Figure 1**

**Step 3.** Repeat Steps 1 and 2 to complete 90 Spider Web blocks.

*TIP*
*When making a totally scrappy quilt, you may want to precut your fabric and randomly sew the pieces together. It is easy to do this if you place the pieces in a bag and pull out pieces one at a time or just stack them up and take the top one. Often we find ourselves trying to coordinate scraps when a really scrappy quilt doesn't require any matching of colors.*

## Completing the Quilt
**Step 1.** Join nine blocks in 10 rows referring to Figure 2 for block arrangements; press seams in adjacent rows in opposite directions.
**Step 2.** Join the rows to complete the pieced center; press seams in one direction.

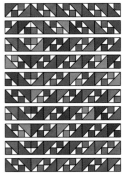

**Figure 2**

**Halloween Spider Web**
Placement Diagram 53" x 58"

**Step 3.** Sew D strips to opposite long sides and E strips to the top and bottom to complete the pieced top; press seams toward D and E strips.

**Step 4.** Finish the quilt referring to the Finishing Instructions on page 168. ◆

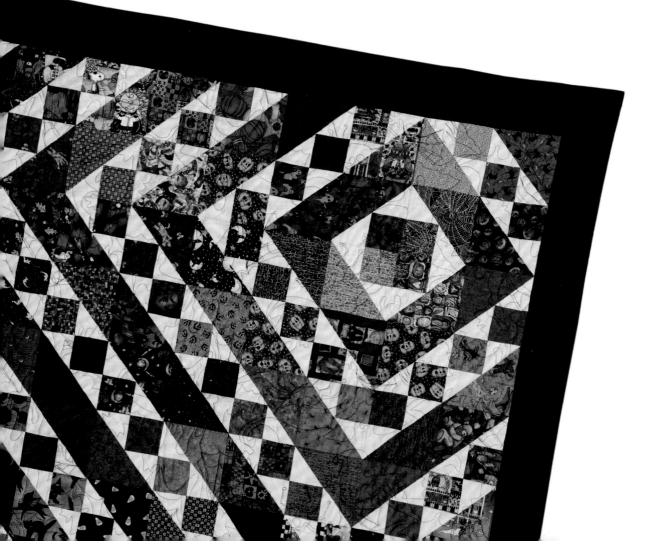

# Scrap-Patch Bed Quilts

Quilts were originally stitched for the practical purpose of making bedcovers that would keep family members warm. Such quilts were both a necessity and a work of love. To many quilters today, bed quilts provide that same opportunity to show their creativity while stitching bed coverings that add a warm, loving touch to any bed the quilt graces. These classic quilt designs will give you lots of opportunities to try your hand at patterns that have stood the test of time.

# Nine-Patch Weave

Design by SUE HARVEY & SANDY BOOBAR

## A collection of 12 coordinated fat quarters makes planning for this quilt very easy.

### Project Specifications

Skill Level: Beginner
Quilt Size: 62½" x 77½"
Block Size: 13½" x 13½"
Number of Blocks: 12

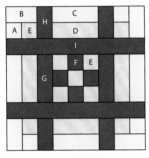

**Dark Grid**
13½" x 13½" Block
Make 6

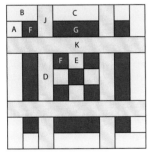

**Light Grid**
13½" x 13½" Block
Make 6

| FABRIC Measurements based on 42" usable fabric width. | #STRIPS & PIECES | CUT | #PIECES | SUBCUT |
|---|---|---|---|---|
| 6 dark fat quarters | 6 | 2" x 21" strips each | 13 | 2" F squares |
| | | | 6 | 5" G rectangles |
| | | | 4 | 3½" H rectangles |
| | | | 2 | 14" I strips |
| 6 light fat quarters | 6 | 2" x 21" strips each | 13 | 2" E squares |
| | | | 6 | 5" D rectangles |
| | | | 4 | 3½" J rectangles |
| | | | 2 | 14" K strips |
| ½ yard aqua print | 6 | 2½" x 42" P/Q | | |
| ⅝ yard diagonal stripe | 7 | 2¼" x 42" binding | | |
| ⅞ yard light aqua print | 13 | 2" x 42" | 48 | 2" A squares |
| | | | 48 | 3½" B rectangles |
| | | | 48 | 5" C rectangles |
| ⅞ yard dark brown print | 3 | 2" x 42" | 8 | 14" L strips |
| | 9 | 2" x 42" M/N/O | | |
| 1½ yards brown floral | 7 | 6½" x 42" R/S | | |
| Backing | | 69" x 84" | | |

### SUPPLIES

- Batting 69" x 84"
- All-purpose thread to match fabrics
- Hand- or machine-quilting thread
- Basic sewing tools and supplies

### Piecing the Blocks

**Step 1.** Select all the cut pieces for one dark fabric and one light fabric.

**Step 2.** To piece one Dark Grid block, arrange five E squares with four F squares in three rows of three squares each as shown in Figure 1. Join the squares in rows; press seams toward F. Join the rows to complete the Nine-Patch center unit; press seams away from the center row.

**Figure 1**

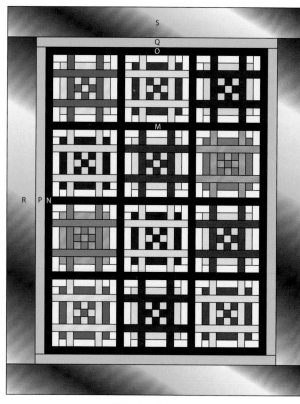

**Nine-Patch Weave**
Placement Diagram 62½" x 77½"

**Step 3.** Sew C to D on the long sides; press seams toward D. Repeat to make four C-D units.

**Step 4.** Sew G to the D side of two C-D units to make two G units as shown in Figure 2;

**Figure 2**

press seams toward G.

**Step 5.** Sew the G units to opposite sides of the Nine-Patch center unit to complete the block center row, again referring to Figure 2; press seams toward the G units.

**Step 6.** Sew A to E; press seam toward E. Add B to complete one corner unit as shown in Figure 3; press seam toward B.

Repeat to make four corner units.

**Figure 3**

**Step 7.** Join two corner units, two H pieces and one C-D unit to make the top block row as shown in Figure 4; press seams toward H. Repeat to make a bottom row.

**Figure 4**

**Step 8.** Join the rows with I strips to complete one Dark Grid block referring to the block drawing for positioning; press seams toward I.

**Step 9.** Repeat Steps 2–8 with the same two fabrics to complete one Light Grid block using A–G, J and K pieces and referring to Figure 5.

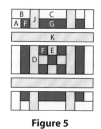

**Figure 5**

**Step 10.** Repeat Steps 1–9 to complete 12 each dark and light blocks.

## Completing the Quilt

**Step 1.** Join one light and two dark blocks with two L strips to complete an X row as shown in Figure 6; press seams toward L.

Repeat to make two X rows.

**Step 2.** Sew one dark and two light blocks with two L strips to make a Y row, again referring to Figure 6; press seams toward L. Repeat to make two Y rows.

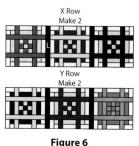

**Figure 6**

**Step 3.** Join the M/N/O strips on the short ends to make one long strip; press seams to one side. Subcut strip into three 44" M strips, two 59" N strips and two 47" O strips.

**Step 4.** Join the X and Y rows with the three M strips to complete the pieced center referring to the Placement Diagram for positioning of rows; press seams toward the M strips.

**Step 5.** Sew the N strips to opposite long sides and O strips to the top and bottom of the pieced center; press seams toward strips.

**Step 6.** Repeat Step 3 with the P/Q strips and subcut into two 62" P strips and two 51" Q strips.

**Step 7.** Repeat Step 3 with the R/S strips and subcut into two 66" R strips and two 63" S strips.

**Step 8.** Repeat Step 5 with the P and Q and R and S strips in alphabetical order; press seams toward each strip as added to complete the pieced top.

**Step 9.** Layer, quilt and bind to complete the quilt referring to the Finishing Instructions on page 168. ◆

# Windowpanes

Design by CATE TALLMAN-EVANS

## Look for scraps in similar color families to make this neutral-color, lap-size quilt.

### Project Specifications
Skill Level: Beginner
Quilt Size: 66" x 78½"
Block Size: 12½" x 12½"
Number of Blocks: 20

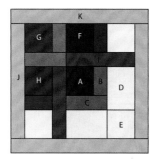

**Windowpanes**
12½" x 12½" Block
Make 20

### Project Notes
The A, F, G and H squares in the blocks in this quilt are all made using the same fabrics in the same position in each block. For a real scrappy look, mix up the pieces to create blocks with a variety of fabric in each place. Keep the value placement the same in each block to separate the dark squares from the light squares and joining pieces.

### Completing the Blocks
**Step 1.** To complete one Windowpanes block, sew B to one side and a matching C to an adjacent side of A to complete an A-B-C unit as shown in Figure 1; press seams toward B and C.

| FABRIC Measurements based on 42" usable fabric width. | #STRIPS & PIECES | CUT | #PIECES | SUBCUT |
|---|---|---|---|---|
| 1 fat quarter each deep brown (A), rust (G), charcoal (F) and brown (H) | 3 | 3" x 21" each fabric | 20 | 3" squares each fabric labeled A, G, F and H (total 80) |
| 4 taupe/brown fat quarters | 5 | 1¾" x 21" each fabric | 10 | 4¼" C rectangles each fabric (total 40) |
| | | | 20 | 3" B rectangles each fabric (total 80) |
| 6 cream tonal fat quarters | 2 | 3" x 21" each fabric | 10 | 3" E squares each fabric (total 60) |
| 4 tan tonal fat quarters | 3 | 3" x 21" each fabric | 10 | 4¼" D rectangles each fabric (total 40) |
| 10 medium print or tonal fat quarters | 6 | 1¾" x 21" | 4 | 10½" J pieces each fabric (total 40) |
| | | | 4 | 13" K pieces each fabric (total 40) |
| ¾ yard dark brown tonal | 8 | 2¼" x 42" binding | | |
| 1 yard rust print | 7 | 1¾" x 42" | 40 | 6¾" I rectangles |
| | 6 | 2½" x 42" L/M | | |
| 1½ yards brown/ rust print | 7 | 6½" x 42" N/O | | |
| Backing | | 72" x 85" | | |

### SUPPLIES
- Batting 72" x 85"
- All-purpose thread to match fabrics
- Quilting thread
- Basic sewing tools and supplies

**Step 2.** Repeat Step 1 with G and matching B and C pieces

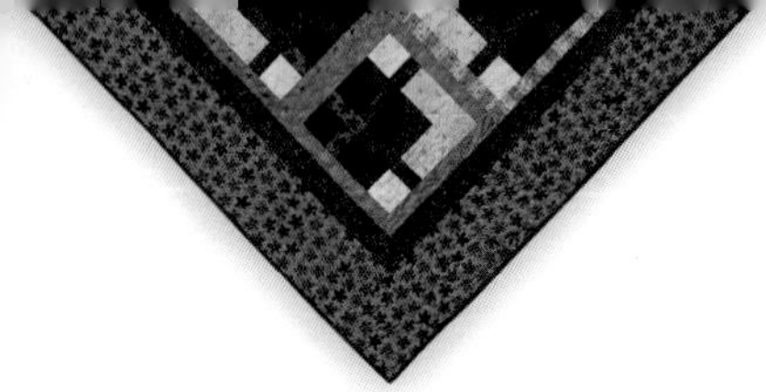



to complete a G-B-C unit, again referring to Figure 1.

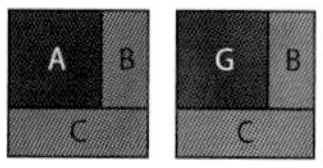


**Figure 1**

**Step 3.** Add D to the A-B-C unit; press seam toward D.

**Step 4.** Sew D to E and add to the A-B-C unit to complete the block corner as shown in Figure 2; press seams toward D and D-E.

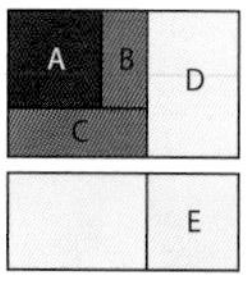


**Figure 2**

**Step 5.** Join one each E and F squares with B; press seams toward B. Sew this unit to the block corner with I as shown in Figure 3; press seams toward I.

*TIP*

*Use block components as leaders and enders when piecing. Units that work well are Nine-Patches, Four-Patches, half-square triangles or flying geese units. After stitching, place in a basket and press when you get a chance.*

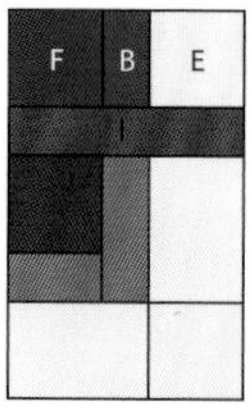


**Figure 3**

**Step 6.** Join one each E and H squares with B and add I as shown in Figure 4; press seams toward B and then I.

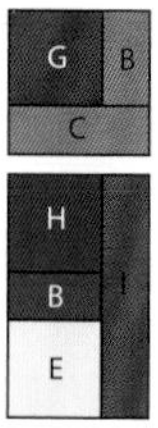


**Figure 4**

**Step 7.** Sew the pieced unit to the C side of the G-B-C unit, again referring to Figure 4; press seam toward the G-B-C unit.

**Step 8.** Join the pieced strips as shown in Figure 5; press seams toward the G side.

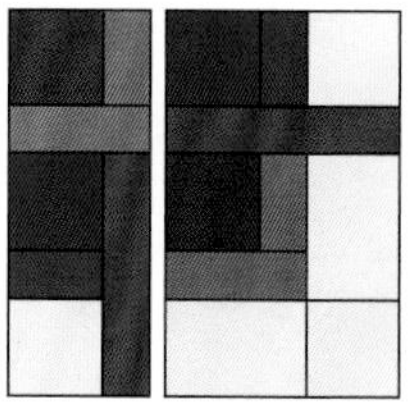

**Figure 5**

**Step 9.** Sew matching J strips to opposite sides and K to the top and bottom of the pieced unit to complete one Windowpanes block referring to

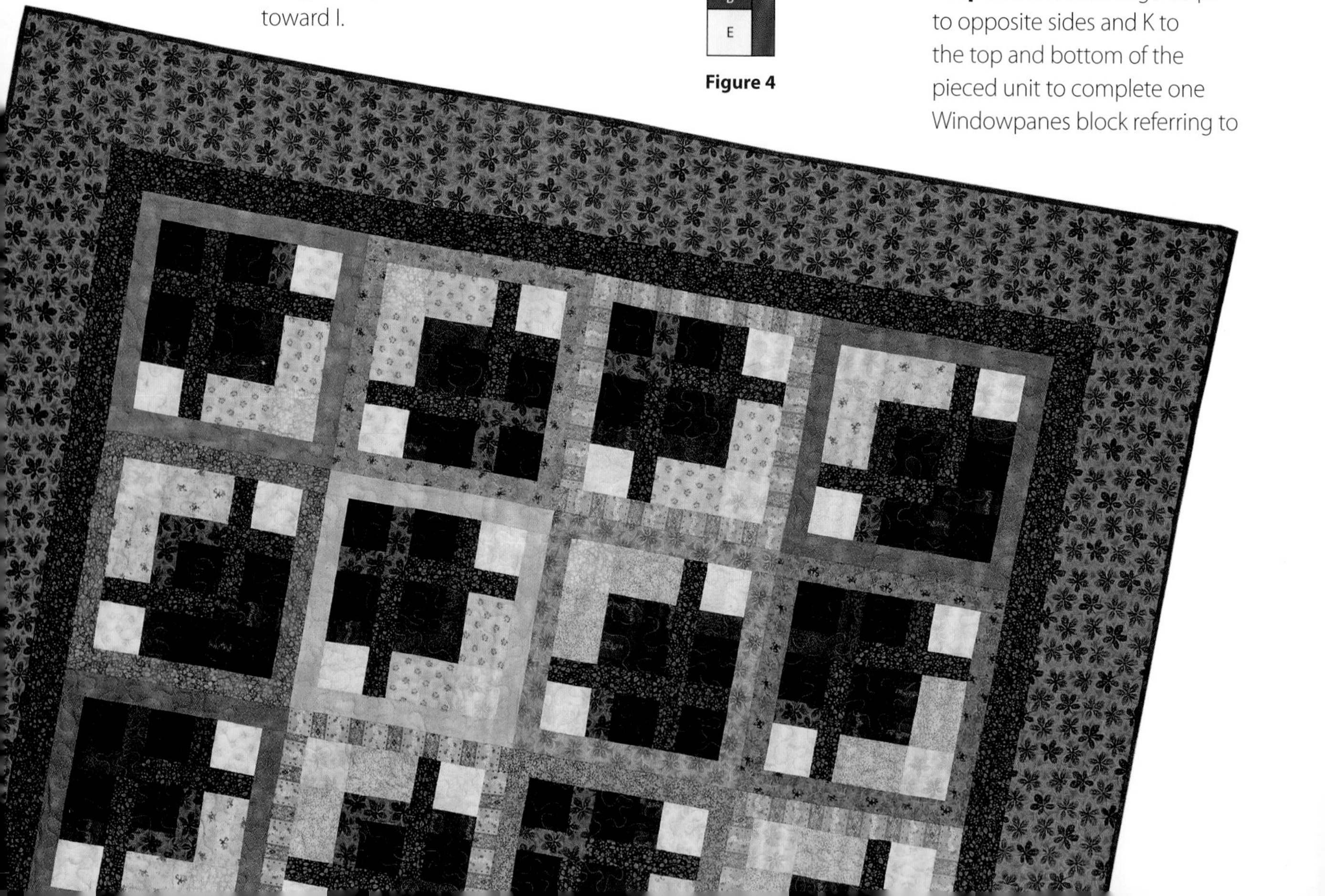

the block drawing; press seams toward J and K strips.

**Step 10.** Repeat Steps 1–9 to complete 20 Windowpanes.

## Completing the Quilt

**Step 1.** Arrange and join four Windowpanes to complete an X row as shown in Figure 6; press seams in one direction. Repeat to make three X rows.

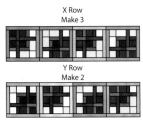

**Figure 6**

**Step 2.** Arrange and join four Windowpanes to complete a Y row, again referring to Figure 6; press seams in opposite direction of X rows. Repeat to make two Y rows.

**Step 3.** Join the rows to complete the pieced center referring to the Placement Diagram for positioning of rows; press seams in one direction.

**Step 4.** Join the L/M strips with right sides together on short ends to make one long strip; press seams open. Subcut strips into two 63" L strips and two 54½" M strips.

**Step 5.** Sew L strips to opposite sides and M strips to the top and bottom of the pieced center; press seams toward L and M strips.

**Step 6.** Join the N/O strips with right sides together on short ends to make one long strip; press seams open. Subcut strips into two 67" N strips and two 66½" O strips.

**Step 7.** Sew N strips to opposite sides and O strips to the top and bottom of the pieced center to complete the pieced top; press seams toward N and O strips.

**Step 8.** Finish the quilt referring to the Finishing Instructions on page 168. ◆

**Windowpanes**
Placement Diagram 66" x 78½"

# Building Blocks

Design by SUE HARVEY & SANDY BOOBAR

A tool-theme print seems appropriate for this quilt design that is made by adding block after block of color around the center squares.

## Project Specifications

Skill Level: Beginner
Quilt Size: 72" x 90"
Block Size: 14" x 14"
Number of Blocks: 12

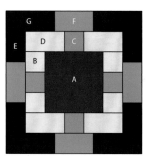

**Building**
14" x 14" Block
Make 12

## Piecing the Blocks

**Step 1.** Sew a C strip between two B strips with right sides together along the length; press seams toward C. Repeat to make two B-C strip sets.

**Step 2.** Cut the B-C strip sets into (24) 2½" B-C units as shown in Figure 1.

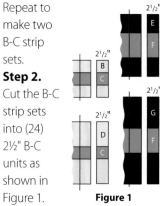

**Figure 1**

| FABRIC Measurements based on 42" usable fabric width. | #STRIPS & PIECES | CUT | #PIECES | SUBCUT |
|---|---|---|---|---|
| Yellow scraps | 4 | 2½" x 42" B | | |
| | 4 | 4½" x 42" D | | |
| Red scraps | 4 | 3½" x 42" E | | |
| | 4 | 5½" x 42" G | | |
| Blue scraps | 6 | 4½" x 42" H | | |
| | 8 | 2¼" x 42" binding | | |
| Green scraps | 4 | 2½" x 42" C | | |
| | 4 | 4½" x 42" F | | |
| | 3 | 6½" x 42" I | | |
| | 28 | 3½" N squares | | |
| 1 yard red bolt print | 8 | 3½" x 42" | 10 | 18½" M strips |
| | | | 4 | 12½" P strips |
| | | | 4 | 9½" O strips |
| 2¼ yards black tool print | 2 | 6½" x 42" | 12 | 6½" A squares |
| | 2 | 4½" x 42" | 6 | 4½" J squares |
| | | | 10 | 2½" K rectangles |
| | | | 4 | 2½" L squares |
| | 8 | 6½" Q/R | | |
| Backing | | 78" x 96" | | |

### SUPPLIES

- Batting 78" x 96"
- All-purpose thread to match fabrics
- Quilting thread
- Basic sewing tools and supplies

### TIP

*Because the design of this quilt depends on the frames of different colors stitched around the center square, it is best to use fabrics that are tonals or very small subtle prints in the blocks. Splashy or multicolored prints will make the frames blend together.*

**Step 3.** Repeat Steps 1 and 2 with C and D strips to cut 24 C-D units, E and F strips to cut 24 E-F units and F and G strips to cut 24 F-G units, again referring to Figure 1.

**Step 4.** To piece one Building block, refer to the block drawing throughout the following steps.

**Step 5.** Sew a B-C unit to opposite sides of A; press seams toward B-C. Repeat with a C-D unit on the remaining sides of A; press seams toward C-D.

**Step 6.** Sew E-F units to opposite sides of the pieced unit; press seams toward E-F. Repeat with F-G units on the remaining sides of the pieced unit to complete the block; press seams toward F-G.

**Step 7.** Repeat Steps 4–6 to make 12 Building blocks.

## Completing the Quilt

**Step 1.** Sew an I strip between two H strips with right sides together along the length; press seams toward H. Repeat to make three I-H strip sets.

*TIP*

*If you don't have fabric-width strips to work with, cut your fabrics into the strip widths instructed in the cutting chart. When joining strips into the strip sets, begin with any-length strips and then just keep adding strips until the joined strip is about 42"–44" long.*

*Cut around the butted strip ends when cutting the strip sets into units. Because there will be more waste with these strip sets, you may need to stitch more than the number called for in the instructions.*

**Step 2.** Cut the I-H strip sets into (17) 4½" sashing strips and (14) 2½" border strips as shown in Figure 2.

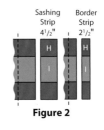

Figure 2

**Step 3.** Join three blocks with two sashing strips and two border strips to make a block row as shown in Figure 3; press seams away from the blocks. Repeat to make four block rows.

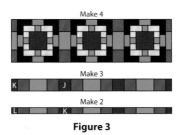

Make 4

Make 3

Make 2

**Figure 3**

**Step 4.** Join three sashing strips with two J squares and two K rectangles to make a sashing row, again referring to Figure 3; press seams toward the sashing strips. Repeat to make three sashing rows.

**Step 5.** Join three border strips with two K rectangles and two L squares to make a border row, again referring to Figure 3;

press seams toward the border strips. Repeat to make two border rows.

**Step 6.** Join the block, sashing and border rows to complete the pieced center referring to the Placement Diagram for positioning; press seams away from the block rows.

**Step 7.** Mark a diagonal line from corner to corner on the wrong side of each N square.

**Step 8.** Place N right sides together on each end of M as shown in Figure 4; stitch on the marked lines, trim seam allowance to ¼" and press N to the right side to complete one M-N unit, again referring to Figure 4. Repeat to make 10 M-N units.

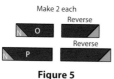

**Figure 4**

**Step 9.** Repeat Step 8 to make two each N-O and reverse N-O units and two each N-P and reverse N-P units as shown in Figure 5.

**Figure 5**

**Step 10.** Join three M-N units with one each N-O and reverse N-O units to make a side border strip as shown in Figure 6; press seams to one side. Repeat to make two side border strips.

**Step 11.** Join two M-N units with one each N-P and reverse N-P units to make an end border strip, again referring to Figure 6; press seams to one side. Repeat to make two end border strips.

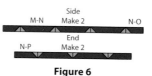

**Figure 6**

**Step 12.** Sew the side border strips to opposite long sides and the end border strips to the top and bottom of the pieced center referring to the Placement Diagram for positioning; press seams toward the pieced center.

**Step 13.** Join the Q/R strips on the short ends to make one long strip; press seams to one side. Subcut the strip into two 78½" Q strips and two 72½" R strips.

**Step 14.** Sew the Q strips to opposite long sides and the R strips to the top and bottom of the pieced center; press seams toward the strips to complete the top.

**Step 15.** Finish the quilt referring to the Finishing Instructions on page 168. ◆

**Building Blocks**
Placement Diagram 72" x 90"

*TIP*

*Store fat quarters in a hanging shoe rack suspended from a closet rod in your sewing room. This makes them all visible while adding a blaze of color to your room's decor. Be careful that sunlight doesn't hit them at any time or they will fade, especially along folded edges.*

# Batik Bonanza

Design by LUCY A. FAZELY & MICHAEL L. BURNS

## Collect lots of batik scraps to make this beautiful bed-size quilt.

### Project Specifications
Skill Level: Intermediate
Quilt Size: 75" x 90"
Block Size: 15" x 15"
Number of Blocks: 30

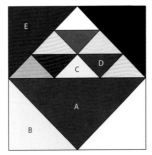

**Batik Bonanza**
15" x 15" Block
Make 30

### Completing the Blocks
**Step 1.** Mark a diagonal line on the wrong side of each B square.

**Step 2.** To complete one Batik Bonanza block, place B on one end of A and stitch on the marked line referring to Figure 1; trim seam to ¼" and press B to the right side.

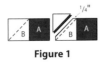

**Figure 1**

**Step 3.** Repeat Step 2 with B on the remaining end of A to complete an A-B unit as shown in Figure 2.

| FABRIC Measurements based on 42" usable fabric width. | #STRIPS & PIECES | CUT | #PIECES | SUBCUT |
|---|---|---|---|---|
| Light-to-medium batik scraps | 30 | 8" B squares | | |
| | 90 | 4⅜" squares | | Cut in half on 1 diagonal to make 180 C triangles |
| Dark batik scraps | 30 | 8" x 15½" A rectangles | | |
| | 30 | 8⅜" squares | | Cut in half on 1 diagonal to make 60 E triangles |
| | 45 | 4⅜" squares | | Cut in half on 1 diagonal to make 90 D triangles |
| ¾ yard black batik | 9 | 2¼" x 42" binding | | |
| Backing | | 81" x 96" | | |

### SUPPLIES
- Batting 81" x 96"
- All-purpose thread to match fabrics
- Quilting thread
- Basic sewing tools and supplies

**Figure 2**

**Step 4.** Sew C to D on the diagonal as shown in Figure 3; press seam toward D. Repeat to make three triangle/squares.

**Figure 3**

**Step 5.** Join the triangle/squares with three C triangles to complete the C-D unit as shown in Figure 4; press seams toward C.

**Figure 4**

**Step 6.** Sew an E triangle to each short side of the C-D unit to

complete the top unit as shown in Figure 5; press seams toward E.

**Figure 5**

**Step 7.** Join the top unit with the A-B unit to complete one Batik Bonanza block referring to the block drawing; press seams toward the A-B unit.

**Step 8.** Repeat Steps 2–7 to complete 30 Batik Bonanza blocks.

## Completing the Quilt

**Step 1.** Arrange and join five blocks to complete a row referring to the Placement Diagram for positioning; press seams in one direction.

**Step 2.** Repeat Step 1 to make six rows, pressing seams in half the rows in one direction and half in the opposite direction.

**Step 3.** Join the rows, alternating seam pressing, to complete the pieced top.

**Step 4.** Finish the quilt referring to the Finishing Instructions on page 168. ◆

*TIP*
*Stitch on the diagonal of the cut-off A-B sections to create triangle/square A-B units to be used in another quilt. It is fun to make a quilt when half the units are already stitched before you start!*

**Batik Bonanza**
Placement Diagram 75" x 90"

# Scraps at the Crossroads

Design by JUDITH SANDSTROM

Select one or two predominant colors, and then look for scraps to match.

## Project Specifications

Skill Level: Beginner
Quilt Size: 63" x 80"
Block Size: 17" x 17"
Number of Blocks: 12

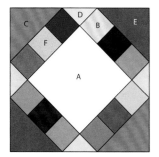

**Crossroads**
17" x 17" Block
Make 12

## Completing the Blocks

**Step 1.** To complete one Crossroads block, join three B squares to make a B strip; press seams in one direction. Repeat to make two B strips.

**Step 2.** Sew a B strip to opposite sides of A and add E as shown in Figure 1; press seams toward A and E.

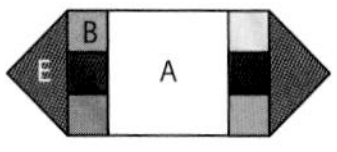

**Figure 1**

**Step 3.** Join three F squares to make an F strip; press seams in

| FABRIC<br>Measurements based on 42" usable fabric width. | #STRIPS & PIECES | CUT | #PIECES | SUBCUT |
|---|---|---|---|---|
| Assorted peach and rust scraps | 152 | 3½" B squares | | |
| Assorted blue and green scraps | 152 | 3½" F squares | | |
| ¾ yard dark green tonal | 3 | 7¼" x 42" | 12 | 7¼" squares; cut in half on 1 diagonal to make 24 E triangles |
| ⅝ yard light blue print | 1<br>2 | 6½" x 42"<br>5½" x 42" | 4<br>12 | 6½" G squares<br>5½" squares; cut on both diagonals to make 48 D triangles |
| 1 yard cream tonal | 3 | 9½" x 42" | 12 | 9½" A squares |
| 1¼ yards deep peach print | 3 | 7¼" x 42" | 12 | 7¼" squares; cut in half on 1 diagonal to make 24 C triangles |
| | 8 | 2¼" x 42" binding | | |
| Backing | | 69" x 86" | | |

## SUPPLIES

- Batting 69" x 86"
- All-purpose thread to match fabrics
- Quilting thread
- Basic sewing tools and supplies

one direction. Repeat to make two F strips.

**Step 4.** Sew D to each end of each F strip and add C to complete a corner unit as shown in Figure 2; press seams toward C and D. Repeat to make two corner units.

**Figure 2**

**Step 5.** Sew a corner unit to opposite sides of the center unit to complete one Crossroads block referring to the block drawing; press seams toward the corner units.

**Step 6.** Repeat Steps 1–5 to complete 12 Crossroads blocks.

## Completing the Quilt

**Step 1.** Join three blocks to make a row; press seams in one direction. Repeat to make four rows.

**Step 2.** Join the rows to complete the pieced center; press seams in one direction.

**Step 3.** Join one each B and F squares to make a B-F unit; press seam to one side. Repeat to make 80 B-F units.

**Step 4.** Join 23 B-F units to make a side strip; press seams in one direction. Trim ½" off each end of the strip. Repeat to make two side strips.

**Step 5.** Sew a side strip to opposite long sides of the pieced center; press seams toward side strips.

**Step 6.** Join 17 B-F units to make the top strip; press seams in one direction. Add a G square to each end. Repeat to make the bottom strip.

**Step 7.** Sew the top and bottom strips to the pieced center; press seams toward top and bottom strips to complete the pieced top.

**Step 8.** Finish the quilt referring to the Finishing Instructions on page 168. ◆

**Scraps at the Crossroads**
Placement Diagram 63" x 80"

## TIP

*When using the trimming-square technique to make flying geese or other quick-pieced units, try sewing another seam ½" away from the first seam and cutting away between the stitched lines to create a stitched triangle/square unit. Use the stitched units to make a matching valance, pillow, sham, pillowcase, etc. It is much easier to stitch them accurately when they are already matched together. Store the stitched units in zipper bags with other scraps from the same project to find easily later.*

# Over & Under

Design by CONNIE RAND

## Make a quilt with matching pillowcases in bright, summery colors.

### Project Specifications
Skill Level: Beginner
Quilt Size: 82" x 82"
Pillowcase Size: 30" x 20"
Block Size: 12" x 12"
Number of Blocks: 27

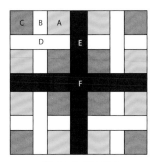

**Over & Under**
12" x 12" Block
Make 25 for quilt
Make 2 for pillowcases

### Over & Under Quilt
#### Completing the Blocks
**Step 1.** Sew a B strip between an A and C strip with right sides together along length; press seams away from B. Repeat to make 27 A-B-C strip sets.

| FABRIC Measurements based on 42" usable fabric width. | #STRIPS & PIECES | CUT | #PIECES | SUBCUT |
|---|---|---|---|---|
| At least 5 assorted yellow fat quarters | 27 | 2½" x 21" | | |
| 1⅛ yards sage green mottled | 7 | 2½" x 42" | 20 | 12½" G strips |
| | 7 | 2½" x 42" H | | |
| | 4 | 4½" x 12½" M | | |
| | 4 | 4½" x 20½" N | | |
| 1⅛ yards red pin dot | 17 | 2" x 42" | 54 | 5¾" E |
| | | | 27 | 12½" F |
| 1⅛ yards grass green mottled | 7 | 2½" x 42" I/J | | |
| 1⅝ yards white tonal | 15 | 1¾" x 42" | 108 | 5¾" D rectangles Cut in half for B |
| | 15 | 1¾" x 42" | | |
| 2⅛ yards pink print | 9 | 2¼" x 42" binding | | |
| | 4 | 2½" x 20½" O | | |
| | 2 | 20½" x 25½" R | | |
| 2⅛ yards floral print | 8 | 5½" x 42" K/L | | |
| | 2 | 5½" x 20½" P | | |
| | 4 | 10½" x 20½" Q | | |
| Backing | | 88" x 88" | | |

### SUPPLIES
- Batting 88" x 88"
- Neutral color all-purpose thread
- Quilting thread
- Basic sewing tools and supplies

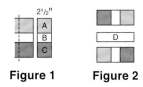

**Figure 1**          **Figure 2**

**Step 2.** Subcut the A-B-C strip sets into (216) 2½" units as shown in Figure 1.

**Step 3.** To complete one Over & Under block, select eight identical A-B-C units. Join two units with a D strip to make a corner unit as shown in Figure 2; press seams toward D. Repeat to make four corner units.

**Step 4.** Join two corner units with E to make a row as shown in Figure 3; press seams toward E. Repeat to make two rows.

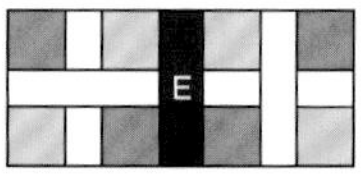

**Figure 3**

**Step 5.** Join the rows with F as shown in Figure 4 to complete one Over & Under block; press seams toward F.

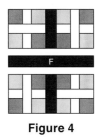

**Figure 4**

**Step 6.** Repeat steps 3–5 to complete 27 blocks; set aside two blocks for the pillowcases.

### Completing the Quilt

**Step 1.** Join five blocks and four G strips to make a row as shown in Figure 5; press seams toward G. Repeat to make five rows.

**Step 2.** Join the H strips with right sides together on short ends to make one long strip; press seams open. Subcut strips into four 68½" H strips.

**Step 3.** Join the rows with the four H strips to complete the quilt center; press seams toward H.

**Step 4.** Join the I/J strips with right sides together on short ends to make one long strip; press seams open. Subcut strip into two 68½" I strips and two 72½" J strips.

**Step 5.** Sew I strips to opposite sides and J strips to the top and bottom of the pieced center; press seams toward I and J strips.

**Step 6.** Join the K/L strips with right sides together on short ends to make one long strip;

press seams open. Subcut the strip into two 72½" K strips and two 82½" L strips.

**Step 7.** Sew K strips to opposite sides and L strips to the top and bottom of the pieced center; press seams toward L and K strips.

**Step 8.** Layer, quilt and bind referring to Finishing Instructions on page 168.

### Over & Under Pillowcases
### Completing the Pillowcases

**Step 1.** To complete one pillowcase, sew M to opposite sides and N to the top and bottom of one previously pieced Over & Under block referring to the Placement Diagram; press seams toward M and N strips.

**Step 2.** Fold O strips with wrong sides together along length; press. Baste an O strip to one long side of one each P and Q strip as shown in Figure 6.

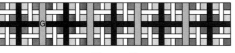

**Figure 5**

**Figure 6**

**Step 3.** Sew an O-P unit to one side of each block and an O-Q unit to the opposite side of the block to complete the pillow-case front as shown in Figure 7; press seams toward O-Q.

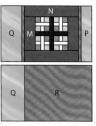

**Figure 7**

**Step 4.** Sew a Q strip to one short side of an R rectangle to complete the pillowcase back, again referring to Figure 7; press seam toward Q.

**Step 5.** Sew the pillowcase back to the pillowcase front on one long side as shown in Figure 8.

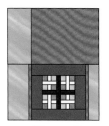

**Figure 8**

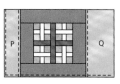

**Figure 9**

**Step 6.** Fold the pillowcase along seam line with right sides together; stitch along the P end and on the long side as shown in Figure 9; press seams flat.

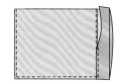

**Figure 10**

**Step 7.** Fold under ¼" on raw edge of Q and press; fold Q to cover the seam between Q and R and O-Q and the block as shown in Figure 10.

**Step 8.** Hand-stitch or topstitch in place to complete the pillowcase.

**Step 9.** Repeat steps 1–8 to complete a second pillowcase. ◆

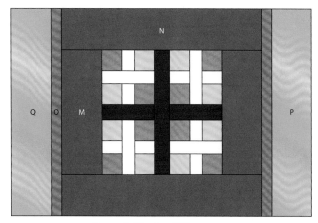

**Over & Under Pillowcase**
Placement Diagram
30" x 20"

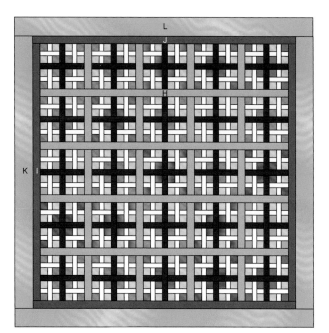

**Over & Under**
Placement Diagram
82" x 82"

# Nature's Kaleidoscope

Quilters today use cotton fabric the majority of the time, so making a "green" ecological project is the norm, especially now that there are more kinds of natural-fiber batting available. More than that, quilts with motifs from the plant or animal worlds are popular designs. Creating a scrappy quilt is about using color to create a special look or feeling. Such quilts are only a reflection of the patchwork of colors that can be seen in nature herself.

# Autumn Leaves Runner

Design by JILL REBER

## Whip up this simple runner in an evening with raw-edge appliqué.

### Project Specifications

Skill Level: Beginner
Runner Size: 41" x 14½"
Block Size: 3½" x 8½"
Number of Blocks: 10

**Leaf**
3½" x 8½" Block
Make 10

| FABRIC<br>Measurements based on 42" usable fabric width. | #STRIPS & PIECES | CUT |
|---|---|---|
| 10–4" x 9" assorted dark A rectangles | | |
| 10–4" x 9" assorted autumn-color scraps | | Appliqué leaf shapes as per pattern |
| 2¼"-wide scrap strips for binding to total 135" when joined | | |
| ⅓ yard border print | 2 | 3½" x 9" B |
| | 2 | 3½" x 41½" C |
| Backing | | 47" x 21" |

### SUPPLIES

- Batting 47" x 21"
- All-purpose thread to match fabrics
- Quilting thread
- Transparent thread
- ¾ yard lightweight fusible web
- Basic sewing tools and supplies

### Completing the Blocks

**Step 1.** Trace 10 leaf shapes onto the paper side of the lightweight fusible web using pattern given; cut out shapes leaving a margin around each one. Remove paper backing.

**Step 2.** Center and fuse a leaf shape to each A rectangle to complete 10 Leaf blocks referring to the block drawing.

*TIP*

*This would be a fun project for a group of quilters to do in an afternoon.*

*• Trade scraps with others to add to your own collection of fabrics.*

*• Use a border print that coordinates with the colors used in your blocks to tie the finished project colors together.*

*• When making a pieced binding of scraps, seam 2¼" strips with diagonal seams and be sure to add at least 12" to the overall amount needed for overlapping beginning and end.*

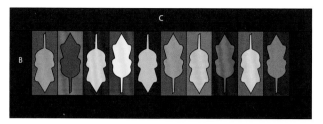

**Autumn Leaves Runner**
Placement Diagram 41" x 14½"

## Completing the Runner

**Step 1.** Arrange and join the 10 Leaf blocks referring to Figure 1; press seams in one direction.

**Figure 1**

**Step 2.** Sew B strips to short ends and C strips to opposite long sides to complete the runner top; press seams toward B and C strips.

**Step 3.** Finish the runner referring to the Finishing Instructions on page 168 and to Figure 10 on page 103 to make binding.

**Step 4.** When quilting and binding is complete, stitch around the inside of each leaf shape and through the center using transparent thread to secure pieces and add quilting at the same time. ◆

**Leaf**
Cut 10 assorted autumn-color scraps

# Colors of Autumn

Design by JODI WARNER

## A myriad of autumn-color scraps mix together in this elegant wall quilt or topper.

### Project Specifications

Skill Level: Intermediate
Quilt Size: 43" x 43"
Block Size: 4½" x 4½"
Number of Blocks: 64

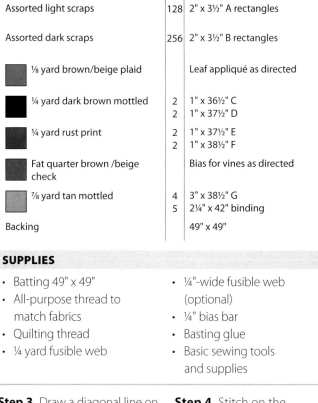

**Autumn Colors**
4¹/₂" x 4¹/₂" Block
Make 64

### Project Notes

This pattern works best when there is an obvious value difference between light and dark pieces. If that contrast is enough, star shapes form at the intersection of four blocks.

### Completing the Blocks

**Step 1.** Arrange rectangles in stacks of light (A) and dark (B).
**Step 2.** Select one each A and B rectangles and layer with right sides together as shown in Figure 1.

**Figure 1**

| FABRIC Measurements based on 42" usable fabric width. | #STRIPS & PIECES | CUT |
|---|---|---|
| Scrap gold dot | 4 | 3" H squares |
| Assorted light scraps | 128 | 2" x 3½" A rectangles |
| Assorted dark scraps | 256 | 2" x 3½" B rectangles |
| ⅛ yard brown/beige plaid | | Leaf appliqué as directed |
| ¼ yard dark brown mottled | 2<br>2 | 1" x 36½" C<br>1" x 37½" D |
| ¼ yard rust print | 2<br>2 | 1" x 37½" E<br>1" x 38½" F |
| Fat quarter brown /beige check | | Bias for vines as directed |
| ⅞ yard tan mottled | 4<br>5 | 3" x 38½" G<br>2¼" x 42" binding |
| Backing | | 49" x 49" |

### SUPPLIES

- Batting 49" x 49"
- All-purpose thread to match fabrics
- Quilting thread
- ¼ yard fusible web
- ¼"-wide fusible web (optional)
- ¼" bias bar
- Basting glue
- Basic sewing tools and supplies

**Step 3.** Draw a diagonal line on the top piece, again referring to Figure 1.

**Figure 2**

**Step 4.** Stitch on the marked line; trim seam allowance to ¼" and press seam toward B, referring to Figure 2.
**Step 5.** Repeat Steps 2–4 to make 128 A-B units and 64 B-B units.

**Step 6.** Join two A-B units with one B-B unit to complete one Autumn Colors block as shown in Figure 3; press seams in one direction. Repeat to complete 64 Autumn Colors blocks.

**Figure 3**

## Completing the Pieced Top

**Step 1.** Arrange and join eight Autumn Colors blocks to make a row as shown in Figure 4; press seams in one direction. Repeat to make eight rows.

**Figure 4**

**Step 2.** Join the rows, turning every other row referring to the Placement Diagram for positioning; press seams in one direction.

**The Colors of Autumn**
Placement Diagram 43" x 43"

**Step 3.** Sew a C strip to opposite sides and D strips to the remaining sides of the pieced center; press seams toward C and D strips.

**Step 4.** Sew an E strip to opposite sides and F strips to the remaining sides of the pieced center; press seams toward E and F strips.

**Step 5.** Sew a G strip to opposite sides of the pieced center; press seams toward G strips.

**Step 6.** Sew an H square to each end of each remaining G strip; press seams toward G.

**Step 7.** Sew a G-H strip to the remaining sides of the pieced center; press seams toward G-H strips.

## Completing the Appliqué

**Step 1.** Transfer vine and leaf positions to H using the Corner Vine & Leaf Layout pattern given.

**Step 2.** Mark the center of each G strip with a pin. Starting at the pinned center of each G strip, transfer the border vine and leaf positions, aligning the centerline on the pattern with the pinned border center, repositioning the pattern section along border to meet the H corners to complete the pattern.

**Step 3.** Cut and prepare 170" of ¼"-wide bias strip from brown/beige check using your favorite method of making bias strips.

**Step 4.** Place bias strip on borders and corners on marked lines around the quilt edges, neatly joining where ends meet; glue-baste or pin to hold in place. Hand-stitch in place.

**Step 5.** Trace 32 leaf shapes onto the paper side of the fusible web; cut out shapes, leaving a margin around each one. Fuse shapes to the wrong side of the brown/beige plaid.

**Step 6.** Cut out shapes on traced lines; arrange and fuse in place along appliquéd vine referring to the vine pattern and Placement Diagram for positioning.

**Step 7.** Machine-appliqué each leaf in place using a short, narrow blanket stitch and matching thread. Pull threads to the back side; tie off to finish.

## Finishing

**Step 1.** Transfer leaf quilting design to the B areas between the star designs formed at block intersections as shown in Figure 5.

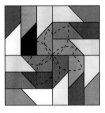

**Figure 5**

**Step 2.** Finish the quilt referring to the Finishing Instructions on page 168. ***Note:*** *The quilt shown was machine-quilted on the marked design lines, in the ditch of seams between blocks and around the formed star design and next to border seams and vine and leaf edges.* ◆

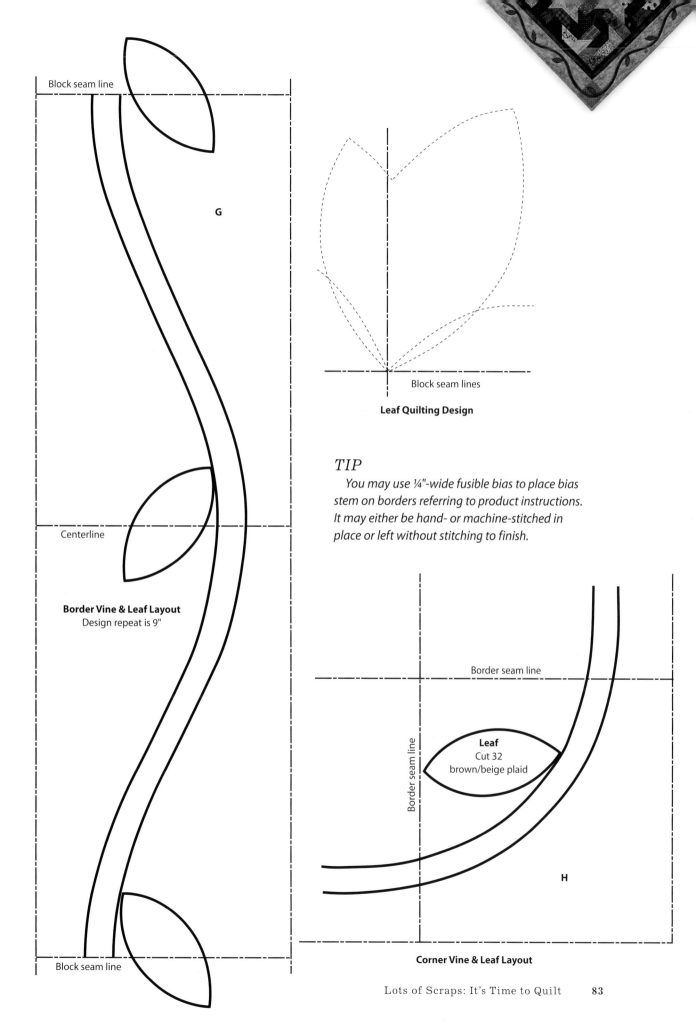

Block seam line

**G**

Centerline

**Border Vine & Leaf Layout**
Design repeat is 9"

Block seam line

Block seam lines

**Leaf Quilting Design**

*TIP*

*You may use ¼"-wide fusible bias to place bias stem on borders referring to product instructions. It may either be hand- or machine-stitched in place or left without stitching to finish.*

Border seam line

Border seam line

**Leaf**
Cut 32
brown/beige plaid

**H**

**Corner Vine & Leaf Layout**

# Falling Leaves

Design by RUTH SWASEY

## Bright orange, gold and brown colors bring autumn leaves inside in this bright-colored bed quilt.

### Project Specifications

Skill Level: Intermediate
Quilt Size: 84" x 96"
Block Size: 12" x 12"
Number of Blocks: 42

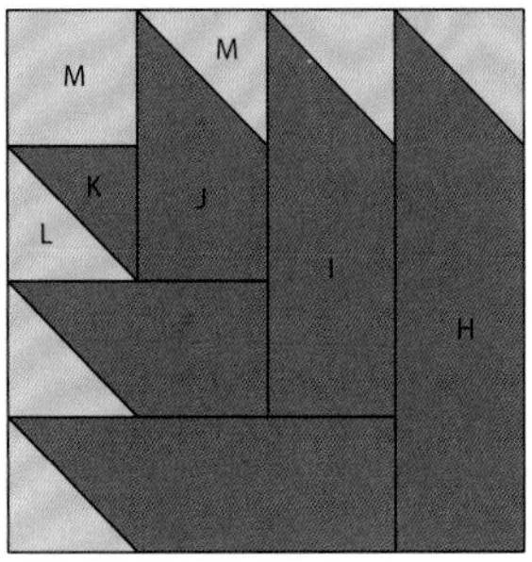

**Large Leaf**
12" x 12" Block
Make 22

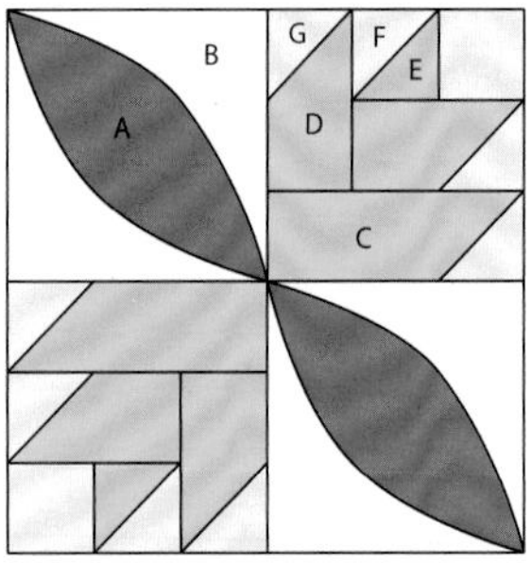

**Small Leaf**
12" x 12" Block
Make 20

### Completing the Large Leaf Blocks

**Step 1.** Set aside 22 M squares. Mark a diagonal line from corner to corner on the wrong side of each remaining M square.

| FABRIC Measurements based on 42" usable fabric width. | #STRIPS & PIECES | CUT | #PIECES | SUBCUT |
|---|---|---|---|---|
| 22 fat quarters leaf fabrics | 1 | 3½" x 12½" H each | | |
| | 2 | 3½" x 9½" I each | | |
| | 2 | 3½" x 6½" J each | | |
| | 1 | 3⅞" square each | | Cut in half on 1 diagonal to make 2 K triangles each |
| | 1 | 2¼" x 21" binding each | | |
| Cream scraps | 11 | 3⅞" squares | | Cut in half on 1 diagonal to make 22 L triangles |
| | 132 | 3½" M squares | | |
| 1 yard cream metallic | 4 | 6⅞" x 42" | 26 | 6⅞" O squares |
| 1⅛ yards cream tonal | 2 | 2⅞" x 42" | 20 | 2⅞" F squares |
| | 10 | 2½" x 42" | 160 | 2½" G squares |
| 1½ yards gold tonal | 3 | 6½" x 42" | 40 | 2½" C pieces |
| | 5 | 4½" x 42" | 80 | 2½" D pieces |
| | 2 | 2⅞" x 42" | 20 | 2⅞" E squares |
| 1⅝ yards cream/tan print | 8 | 6½" x 42" | 44 | 6½" B squares |
| 2 yards red-orange floral | 4 | 6⅞" x 42" A pieces as per pattern | 26 | 6⅞" N squares |
| Backing | | 90" x 102" | | |

### SUPPLIES

- Batting 90" x 102"
- All-purpose thread to match fabrics
- Quilting thread
- 1⅞ yards 18"-wide fusible web
- 2½ yards fabric stabilizer
- Basic sewing tools and supplies

**Step 2.** Select matching J, K, H and I pieces, one unmarked and five marked M squares and one L triangle.

**Step 3.** Place a marked M square right sides together with an H rectangle and stitch on the marked line as shown in Figure 1. Trim seam to ¼"; press seam toward M.

**Figure 1**

**Step 4.** Repeat Step 3 to complete one each M-I, reverse M-I, M-J and reverse M-J units as shown in Figure 2.

**Figure 2**

**Step 5.** To complete one Large Leaf block, sew K to L along the diagonal; press seam in one direction. Discard one K triangle each fabric.

**Step 6.** Sew the unmarked M square to the K-L unit as shown in Figure 3; press seam toward M.

Figure 3     Figure 4

**Step 7.** Sew an M-J and reverse M-J unit to two adjacent sides of the M-K-L unit as shown in Figure 4; press seams toward M-J units.

**Step 8.** Repeat Step 5 with M-I, reverse M-I and M-H units as shown in Figure 5 to complete one Large Leaf block; press seams toward the M-I and M-H units.

**Figure 5**

**Step 9.** Repeat Steps 2–7 to complete 22 Large Leaf blocks.

## Completing the Small Leaf Blocks

**Step 1.** Mark a diagonal line from corner to corner on the wrong side of all but 40 G squares.

**Step 2.** Place a G square right sides together on D and stitch on the marked line as shown in Figure 6; trim seam to ¼" and press G to the right side to complete a D-G unit.

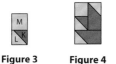   

**Figure 6**     **Figure 7**

**Step 3.** Repeat Step 2 to complete 40 each D-G, reverse D-G and C-G units referring to Figure 7.

**Step 4.** To complete one leaf unit, sew E to F on the diagonal and add G as shown in Figure 8; press seams toward E and G.

Figure 8     Figure 9

**Step 5.** Add a D-G and reverse D-G unit to two adjacent sides of the G-E-F unit as shown in Figure 9; press seams toward the D-G units.

**Step 6.** Add a C-G unit to one side to complete one leaf unit referring to the block drawing; press seam toward the C-G unit.

**Step 7.** Repeat Steps 4–6 to complete 40 leaf units.

**Step 8.** Trace the A shape onto the paper side of the fusible web referring to the pattern for

number to cut; cut out shapes, leaving a margin around each one.

**Step 9.** Fuse A shapes to the wrong side of the red-orange floral; cut out shapes on traced lines.

**Step 10.** Fuse an A shape on the diagonal of a B square as shown in Figure 10.

**Figure 10**

**Step 11.** Cut (44) 4" x 9½" rectangles fabric stabilizer.

**Step 12.** Pin a fabric-stabilizer rectangle to the wrong side of each fused A-B square. Machine-appliqué A shapes in place using matching thread and a machine satin stitch.

**Step 13.** When appliqué is complete, remove fabric stabilizer. Set aside four A-B units for border corners.

**Step 14.** To complete one Small Leaf block, join one each leaf and A-B units to make a row as shown in Figure 11; press seam toward the A-B unit. Repeat to make two rows.

**Figure 11**

**Step 15.** Join the rows to complete one Small Leaf block referring to the block drawing; press seam in one direction.

**Step 16.** Repeat Steps 14 and 15 to complete 20 Small Leaf blocks.

## Completing the Quilt

**Step 1.** Arrange and join the blocks in seven rows of six blocks each referring to the Placement Diagram for positioning of blocks; press seams in adjacent rows in opposite directions.

**Step 2.** Join the rows to complete the pieced center; press seams in one direction.

**Step 3.** Draw a diagonal line from corner to corner on the wrong side of each O square.

**Step 4.** Place an N square right sides together with an O square and stitch ¼" on each side of the marked line as shown in Figure 12.

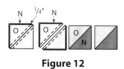

**Figure 12**

**Step 5.** Cut apart on the marked line and press seam toward N to complete two N-O units. Repeat with all N and O squares to complete 52 N-O units.

**Step 6.** Join 12 N-O units referring to the Placement Diagram to make a 12-unit row; press seams in one direction. Repeat to make two 12-unit rows, again referring to the Placement Diagram. Repeat with 14 N-O units to make two 14-unit rows.

**Step 7.** Sew an A-B unit to opposite ends of each 12-unit row to make two A-B rows, again referring to the Placement Diagram; press seams toward the A-B units.

**Step 8.** Sew a 14-unit row to opposite long sides of the pieced center; press seams toward the rows. Sew an A-B row to the top and bottom of the pieced center to complete the pieced top; press seams toward the A-B rows.

**Step 9.** Finish the quilt referring to the Finishing Instructions on page 168. ◆

**Falling Leaves**
Placement Diagram 84" x 96"

**A**
Cut 44 red/orange floral

# March of the Crabs

Design by LUCY A. FAZELY & MICHAEL L. BURNS

## The crabs in the pieced blocks look like they are marching to music on this playful quilt.

### Project Specifications

Skill Level: Intermediate
Quilt Size: 52" x 62"

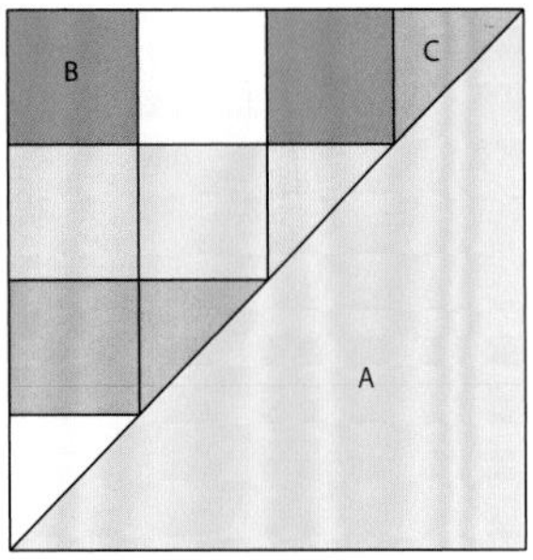

**Triangle**
10" x 10" Block
Make 14

**Crab**
10" x 10" Block
Make 6

| FABRIC<br>Measurements based on 42" usable fabric width. | #STRIPS & PIECES | CUT | #PIECES | SUBCUT |
|---|---|---|---|---|
| 6—9" x 15" scraps red prints | 1 | 5½" D square | | |
| | 1 | 3" x 15" strip each scrap for H and HR | | |
| Assorted tan, beige, cream and gold scraps | 84 | 3" B squares | | |
| | 28 | 3⅜" squares | | Cut in half on 1 diagonal to make 56 C triangles |
| ½ yard black solid | 5 | 2½" x 42" K/L | | |
| 1¼ yards blue print | 6 | 4½" x 42" M/N | | |
| | 6 | 2¼" x 42" binding | | |
| 1½ yards tan dot | 3 | 10⅞" x 42" | 7 | 10⅞" squares; cut in half on 1 diagonal to make 14 A triangles |
| | 1 | 5½" x 42" | 12 | 3" J rectangles |
| | 3 | 3" x 42" | 30 | 3" F squares |
| | 1 | 1¾" x 42" | 6 | 1¾" E squares |
| | | Cut G and I pieces as per templates | | |
| Backing | | 58" x 68" | | |

### SUPPLIES

- Batting 58" x 68"
- All-purpose thread to match fabrics
- Quilting thread
- 12 (⅝") black buttons
- Basic sewing tools and supplies

### Completing the Crab Blocks

**Step 1.** Prepare templates using patterns given; cut as directed on each one, cutting H pieces from the previously cut 3" x 15" red-scrap strips.

**Step 2.** Mark a diagonal line on the wrong side of each E square and six F squares.

**Step 3.** Referring to Figure 1, place an E square right sides together on one corner of D and stitch on the marked line; trim seam to ¼" and press E to the right side.

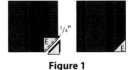

**Figure 1**

**Step 4.** Repeat Step 3 with F on the opposite corner of D to complete the center unit as

shown in Figure 2; repeat to make six center units.

**Figure 2**　　　**Figure 3**

**Step 5.** Sew matching H and HR pieces to G to complete a G-H unit as shown in Figure 3; press seams toward H and HR. Repeat to make 12 G-H units.

**Step 6.** Sew matching H and HR pieces to I to complete a corner unit as shown in Figure 4; press seams toward H and HR. Repeat to make 12 corner units.

**Figure 4**　　　**Figure 5**

**Step 7.** To complete one Crab block, choose one center, two G-H and two corner units of one red fabric. Sew F to a G-H unit to make a side unit as shown in Figure 5; repeat to make two side units. Press seams toward F.

**Step 8.** Sew a side unit and J to opposite sides of the center unit to complete the center row as shown in Figure 6; press seams away from the center unit.

**Figure 6**

**Step 9.** Sew an F square and a corner unit to the remaining side unit to make the top row as shown in Figure 7; press seams toward F.

**Figure 7**

**Step 10.** Join one each F and J with one corner unit to make the bottom row as shown in Figure 8; press seams toward J.

**Figure 8**

**Step 11.** Sew the top and bottom rows to the center row to complete one Crab block referring to the block drawing for positioning; press seams toward the top and bottom rows.

**Step 12.** Repeat Steps 7–11 to complete six Crab blocks.

## Completing the Triangle Blocks

**Step 1.** Arrange and join six B squares and four C triangles to make rows as shown in Figure 9; press seams in adjoining rows in opposite directions.

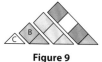

**Figure 9**

**Step 2.** Join the rows as arranged and stitched in Step 1 to complete a B-C unit as shown in Figure 10; press seams in one direction.

**Figure 10**

**Step 3.** Sew a B-C unit to A to complete one Triangle block; press seam toward A.

**Step 4.** Repeat Steps 1–3 to complete 14 Triangle blocks.

## Completing the Quilt

**Step 1.** Arrange the Triangle and Crab blocks in five rows of five blocks each referring to the Placement Diagram for positioning of blocks in each row.

**Step 2.** Join the blocks in rows as arranged; press seams in adjacent rows in opposite directions.

**Step 3.** Join the rows as arranged to complete the pieced center; press seams in one direction.

**Step 4.** Join the K/L strips on short ends to complete one long strip; press seams open. Subcut strip into two 50½" K strips and two 44½" L strips.

**Step 5.** Sew a K strip to opposite long sides and L strips to the top and bottom of the pieced center; press seams toward K and L strips.

**Step 6.** Join the M/N strips on short ends to make one long strip; press seams open. Subcut strip into two 54½" M strips and two 52½" N strips.

**Step 7.** Sew the M strips to opposite long sides and N strips to the top and bottom of the pieced center to complete the top; press seams toward M and N strips.

**Step 8.** Finish the quilt referring to the Finishing Instructions on page 168.

**Figure 11**

**Step 9.** Stitch two black buttons to the D pieces in each Crab block for eyes referring to Figure 11 for positioning to complete the quilt. ◆

*TIP*

• *Make a controlled scrap quilt by using yardage for the background and border strips to cut down on the number of scraps needed. The tan dot used in this quilt's background helps to unify all the red and tan scraps.*

• *When cutting scraps, I always cut more than I actually need to complete my project. This gives me more of a selection when it comes to piecing the last block. If you cut exactly the number needed, you may end up with too many like pieces in the final units or blocks sewn.*

• *Don't be afraid to use novelty prints if the coloring is right. Although this quilt has a beach theme, the fabric scraps used include a paw print, a winter scene and snowflake, sailboat and African-themed prints. Mixed with tonals, small prints and paisleys, it is hard to pick them out unless you look closely. When you do, it is fun to see what you can find.*

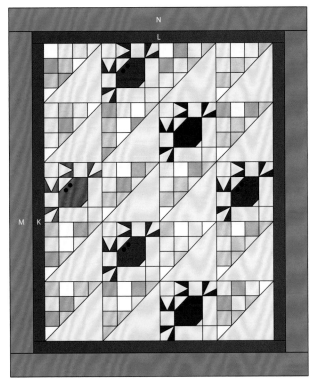

**March of the Crabs**
Placement Diagram 52" x 62"

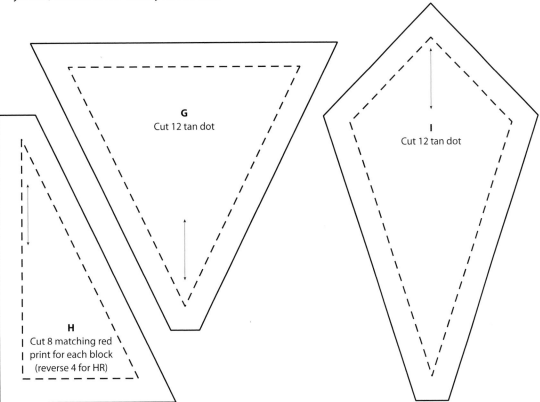

G
Cut 12 tan dot

I
Cut 12 tan dot

H
Cut 8 matching red print for each block (reverse 4 for HR)

# Marvelous Maple

Design by JUDITH SANDSTROM

## Use the same fabrics in the same parts of each block to create a coordinated look in this scrappy twin-size quilt.

### Project Specifications

Skill Level: Intermediate
Quilt Size: 66" x 90"
Block Size: 12" x 12"
Number of Blocks: 35

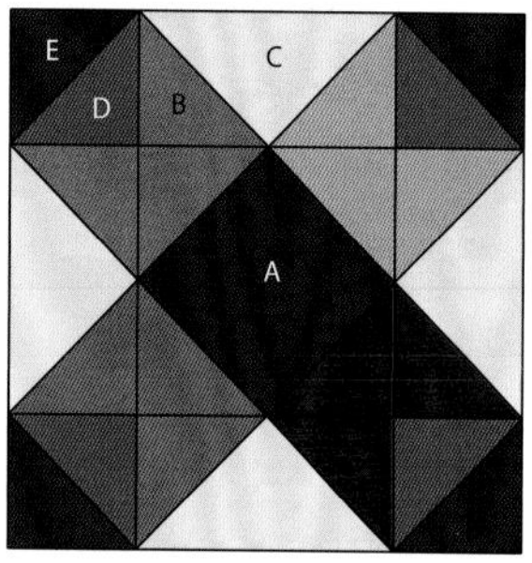

**Diagonal Square**
12" x 12" Block
Make 18

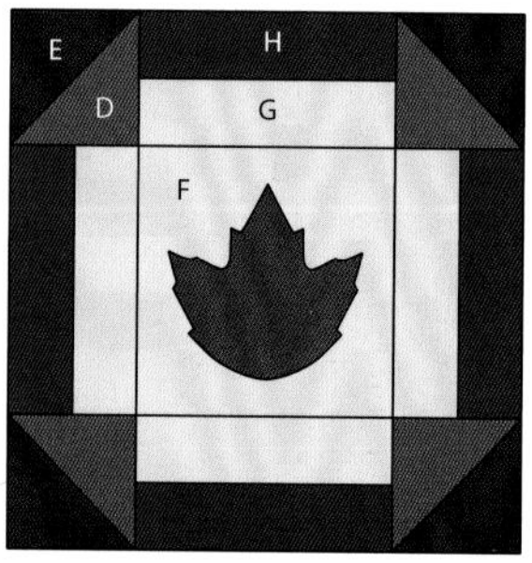

**Leaf**
12" x 12" Block
Make 17

### Completing the Leaf Blocks

**Step 1.** Trace the leaf shape given on page 173 onto the paper side of the fusible web; cut out shapes, leaving a margin around each one.

| FABRIC Measurements based on 42" usable fabric width. | #STRIPS & PIECES | CUT | #PIECES | SUBCUT |
|---|---|---|---|---|
| 17—5" squares assorted leaf-color prints | | Appliqué pieces as per pattern | | |
| 18 or more 4" x 12" assorted autumn-colored rectangles | 3 | 3⅞" squares each rectangle | | Cut in half on 1 diagonal to make a total of 216 B triangles in 72 sets of 3 matching triangles |
| ⅔ yard green print | 8 | 2¼" x 42" binding | | |
| ⅞ yard dark green tonal | 7 | 3⅞" x 42" | 70 | 3⅞" D squares |
| ⅞ yard dark green print | 12 | 2" x 42" H | | |
| 1 yard autumn-leaf print | 8 | 3½" x 42" I/J | | |
| 1⅓ yards dark brown print | 3 | 4¾" x 42" | 18 | 4¾" A squares |
| | 7 | 3⅞" x 42" | 70 | 3⅞" E squares |
| 2⅛ yards cream tonal | 3 | 6½" x 42" | 17 | 6½" F squares |
| | 4 | 7¼" x 42" | 18 | 7¼" squares; cut on both diagonals to make 72 C triangles |
| | 12 | 2" x 42" G | | |
| Backing | | 72" x 96" | | |

### SUPPLIES

- Batting 72" x 96"
- All-purpose thread to match leaf fabrics
- Quilting thread
- ¾ yard 18"-wide fusible web
- 1 yard fabric stabilizer
- Basic sewing tools and supplies

**Step 2.** Fuse shapes to the wrong side of the assorted leaf-color squares; cut out shapes on traced lines. Remove paper backing.

**Step 3.** Fold each F square to mark the horizontal and vertical centers.

**Step 4.** Center and fuse a leaf shape on each F square.

**Step 5.** Cut (17) 5½" x 5½" squares fabric stabilizer; pin a square to the wrong side of each fused F square.

**Step 6.** Using thread to match fabrics and a machine satin stitch, stitch all around each fused leaf. When stitching is complete, remove fabric stabilizer.

**Step 7.** Sew a G strip to an H strip with right sides together along length; press seams toward the H strip. Repeat to make 12 strip sets.

**Step 8.** Subcut strip sets into (68) 6½" G-H units as shown in Figure 1.

**Figure 1**

**Step 9.** Mark a diagonal line on the wrong side of each D square.

**Step 10.** Place a D square right sides together with an E square and stitch ¼" on each side of the marked line as shown in Figure 2.

**Figure 2**

**Step 11.** Cut apart on the marked line to make two D-E units as shown in Figure 3; press seams toward E. Repeat to complete 140 D-E units. Set aside 72 units for the Diagonal Square blocks.

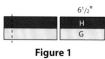

**Figure 3**

**Step 12.** To complete one Leaf block, sew a G-H unit to opposite sides of a fused F square to complete the center row as shown in Figure 4; press seams toward the G-H units.

**Figure 4**

**Step 13.** Sew a D-E unit to opposite ends of a G-H unit to make the top row as shown in Figure 5; repeat to make the bottom row. Press seams toward the G-H units.

**Figure 5**

**Step 14.** Sew the top and bottom rows to the center row referring to the block drawing to complete one Leaf block; press seams away from the center row.

**Step 15.** Repeat Steps 12–14 to complete 17 Leaf blocks.

## Completing the Diagonal Square Blocks

**Step 1.** Select four sets of three matching B triangles.

**Step 2.** To complete one Diagonal Square block, sew one of each B triangles to A as shown in Figure 6; press seams toward B.

**Figure 6**

**Step 3.** To avoid confusion with the placement of the remaining B triangles, arrange four previously pieced D-E units with C and the remaining B triangles in rows around the A-B unit as shown in Figure 7.

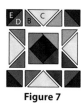

**Figure 7**

**Step 4.** Sew a B triangle to each short side of each C triangle as arranged; press seams toward B.

**Step 5.** Place the stitched units back in the arranged rows and sew a B-C unit to opposite sides of the A-B unit to complete the center row as shown in Figure 8; press seams toward the A-B unit.

**Figure 8**

**Step 6.** Sew a D-E unit to each end of each remaining B-C unit, keeping pieces as arranged, to complete the top and bottom rows as shown in Figure 9; press seams toward the D-E units.

**Figure 9**

**Step 7.** Join the rows as arranged to complete one Diagonal Square block; press seams toward the center row.

**Step 8.** Repeat Steps 2–7 to complete 18 Diagonal Square blocks.

## Completing the Quilt

**Step 1.** Join two Leaf blocks with three Diagonal Square blocks to make an X row as shown in Figure 10; press seams toward Leaf blocks. Repeat to make four X rows.

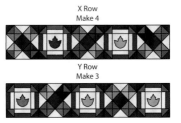

X Row
Make 4

Y Row
Make 3

**Figure 10**

**Step 2.** Join two Diagonal Square blocks with three Leaf blocks to make a Y row, again referring to Figure 10; press seams toward Leaf blocks. Repeat to make three Y rows.

**Step 3.** Join the X and Y rows to complete the pieced top referring to the Placement Diagram for positioning of rows; press seams in one direction.

**Step 4.** Join the I/J strips with right sides together on short ends to make one long strip; press seams open. Subcut strip into two 84½" I strips and two 66½" J strips.

**Step 5.** Sew I strips to opposite sides and J strips to the top and bottom of the pieced center to complete the quilt top; press seams toward I and J strips.

**Step 6.** Finish the quilt referring to the Finishing Instructions on page 168. ◆

**Marvelous Maple**
Placement Diagram 66" x 90"

## *TIP*

*Sew strips of fabric from one color together in one long strip or piece, and use to cut shapes or strips.*

# Under the Apple Tree

Design by CATE TALLMAN-EVANS

Red mixed with green makes the apples stand out on these fabric apple trees.

## Project Specifications

Skill Level: Beginner
Quilt Size: 61" x 61"
Block Size: 13½" x 13½"
Number of Blocks: 5

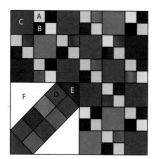

**Apple Tree**
13½" x 13½" Block
Make 5

## Completing the Blocks

**Step 1.** Sew an A strip to a B strip with right sides together along the length to make an A-B strip set; press seams toward B. Repeat to make 12 A-B strip sets.

**Step 2.** Subcut A-B strip sets into (130) 1⅝" A-B segments as shown in Figure 1.

1⅝"

**Figure 1**     **Figure 2**

**Step 3.** Join two A-B segments to make an A-B unit as shown in Figure 2; press seam in one

| FABRIC Measurements based on 42" usable fabric width. | #STRIPS & PIECES | CUT | #PIECES | SUBCUT |
|---|---|---|---|---|
| 6 fat eighths assorted red fabrics | 2 | 1⅝" x 21" B strips each | | |
| 6 fat eighths assorted light green fabrics | 2 | 1⅝" x 21" A strips each | | |
| 6 fat eighths assorted dark green fabrics | 2 | 2¾" x 21" strips each | 70 | 2¾" C squares total |
| 6 fat eighths assorted brown fabrics | 5 | 3⅛" squares total; cut on 1 diagonal to make 10 E triangles | | |
| | 1 | 2⅛" x 21" D strip each | | |
| | 2 | 2⅛" H squares each | | |
| ½ yard dark green tonal | 5 | 2½" x 42" K/L | | |
| ⅝ yard dark red print | 7 | 2¼" x 42" binding | | |
| 1¼ yards cream mottled | 1 | 22⅝" x 42" | 1 | 22⅝" square; cut on both diagonals to make 4 I triangles |
| | | | 5 | 5⅜" squares; cut in half on 1 diagonal to make 10 F triangles |
| | 1 | 12¾" x 42" | 2 | 12¾" squares; cut in half on 1 diagonal to make 4 J triangles |
| 1⅞ yards dark gold tonal | 2 | 6" x 50½" M strips along length | | |
| | 2 | 6" x 61½" N strips along length | | |
| | 4 | 2⅛" strips along length | 16 | 14" G strips |
| Backing | | 67" x 67" | | |

### SUPPLIES
- Batting 67" x 67"
- All-purpose thread to match fabrics
- Quilting thread
- Basic sewing tools and supplies

direction. Repeat to make 65 A-B units.

**Step 4.** Join two D strips with right sides together along the length to make a D strip set; press seam in one direction. Repeat to make six strip sets.

**Step 5.** Subcut the D strip sets into (20) 2⅛" D units as shown in Figure 3.

2⅛"

**Figure 3**

**Step 6.** To complete one Apple Tree block, arrange and join three A-B units with three C squares to make a row as shown in Figure 4; repeat to make three A-B-C rows. Press seams toward C.

**Figure 4**

**Step 7.** Join the A-B-C rows as shown in Figure 5 to complete the top half of the block; press seams in one direction.

**Figure 5**

**Step 8.** Sew C to opposite sides of an A-B unit to make the top row as shown in Figure 6; press seams toward C. Repeat to make a bottom row. Repeat with one C and two A-B units to make the center row, again referring to Figure 6; press seams toward C.

**Figure 6**

**Step 9.** Join the rows to complete the bottom tree section, again referring to Figure 6; press seams in one direction.

**Step 10.** Join four D units to make a strip as shown

### TIP

*When making a quilt with a wide variety of scraps, choose one color for the background color. This ties the quilt together. The background can be all one fabric or a variety of scraps of the same color.*

in Figure 7; press seams in one direction.

**Figure 7**

**Step 11.** Sew E to opposite ends of the D strip and add F to opposite sides to make a tree base unit, again referring to Figure 7; press seams toward E and F.

**Step 12.** Sew the bottom tree section to the tree base unit to complete the block bottom as shown in Figure 8; press seam away from the tree base unit.

**Figure 8**

**Step 13.** Join the top half of the block to the block bottom to complete one Apple Tree block as shown in Figure 9; press seam in one direction.

**Figure 9**

**Step 14.** Repeat Steps 6–13 to complete five Apple Tree blocks.

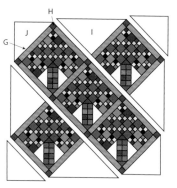

**Figure 10**

### Completing the Quilt

**Step 1.** Arrange and join the blocks with G, H, J and I in diagonal rows as shown in Figure 10 to complete the pieced center; press seams toward G, I and J.

**Step 2.** Join the K/L strips on short ends to make one long strip; press seams open. Subcut strip into two 46½" K strips and two 50½" L strips.

**Step 3.** Sew K strips to opposite sides and L strips to the top and bottom of the pieced center; press seams toward K and L strips.

**Step 4.** Sew M strips to opposite sides and N strips to the top and bottom of the pieced center; press seams toward M and N strips.

**Step 5.** Finish the quilt referring to the Finishing Instructions on page 168. ◆

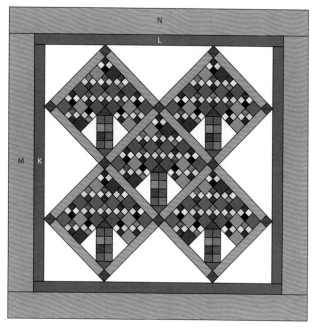

**Under the Apple Tree**
Placement Diagram 61" x 61"

# Happy Scrappy Living

If you don't have much time or if this is your first scrappy project, you might want to start with something small. Even if you are just starting to quilt, you probably have enough scraps to make a scrappy table runner for your home. For a quick project, make a place mat or two. Other small projects you can make in a weekend are a growth chart for a child's bedroom or a tea cozy for the dining area.

# Jacob's Ladder Runner

Design by JILL REBER

## Cream, green, red and navy scraps combine to make this pretty runner.

### Project Specifications
Skill Level: Beginner
Runner Size: 32" x 16"
Block Size: 6" x 6"
Number of Blocks: 8

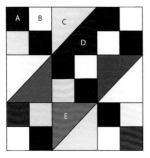

**Jacob's Ladder**
6" x 6" Block
Make 8

| FABRIC<br>Measurements based on 42" usable fabric width. | #STRIPS & PIECES | CUT |
|---|---|---|
| Cream/tan scraps | 16 | 1½"-wide B strips to total 180"<br>2⅞" C squares |
| Red scraps | | 1½"-wide A strips to total 180" |
| Navy scraps | 8 | 2⅞" D squares |
| Green scraps | 8 | 2⅞" E squares<br>2¼"-wide strips to total 120" for binding |
| ½ yard gold print | 2<br>2 | 2½" x 32½" F strips<br>4½" x 12½" E strips |
| Backing | | 38" x 22" |

### SUPPLIES
- Batting 38" x 22"
- All-purpose thread to match fabrics
- Quilting thread
- Basic sewing tools and supplies

### Completing the Blocks

**Step 1.** Join the A strips on the short ends to make four 1½" x 42" strips; repeat with B strips. Press seams open.

**Step 2.** Sew an A strip to a B strip with right sides together along length to make an A-B strip set; repeat to make four strip sets. Press seams toward A strips.

**Step 3.** Subcut the A-B strip sets into (80) 1½" A-B segments as shown in Figure 1. **Note:** *Skip seamed areas when cutting segments, again referring to Figure 1.*

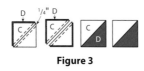

**Figure 1**

**Step 4.** Join two A-B segments as shown in Figure 2 to make an A-B unit; press seam in one direction. Repeat to make 40 A-B units.

**Figure 2**

**Step 5.** Mark a diagonal line from corner to corner on the wrong side of each C square.

**Step 6.** Layer a C square with a D square with right sides together; stitch ¼" on each side of the marked line and cut apart on the marked line as shown in Figure 3; press open with seam toward D. Repeat to make 16 C-D units.

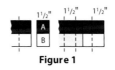

**Figure 3**

**Step 7.** Repeat Step 6 with C and E squares to make 16 C-E units referring to Figure 4.

**Figure 4**

**Step 8.** Sew an A-B unit to two opposite sides of a C-D unit as shown in Figure 5 to make the top row; press seams toward the A-B units.

**Figure 5**

**Step 9.** Sew an A-B unit to two opposite sides of a C-E unit as shown in Figure 6 to make the bottom row; press seams toward the A-B units.

**Figure 6**

**Step 10.** Sew a C-D unit to one side and a C-E unit to the opposite side of an A-B unit to complete the center row as shown in Figure 7; press seams toward the A-B units.

**Figure 7**

**Step 11.** Join the rows as shown in Figure 8 to complete one Jacob's Ladder block; press seams in one direction.

**Figure 8**

**Step 12.** Repeat Steps 8–11 to complete eight Jacob's Ladder blocks.

**Completing the Quilt**

**Step 1.** Arrange and join four blocks to make a row as shown in Figure 9; press seams in one direction. Repeat to make two rows.

**Figure 9**

**Step 2.** Join the rows with seams going in opposite directions to complete the runner center; press seam in one direction.

**Step 3.** Sew F strips to opposite short ends and G to opposite long sides of the runner center to complete the pieced top; press seams toward F and G strips.

**Step 4.** Finish the runner referring to the Finishing Instructions on page 168. ◆

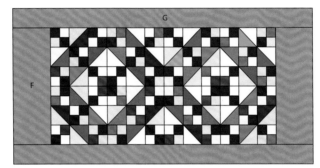

**Jacob's Ladder Runner**
Placement Diagram 32" x 16"

*TIPS*

• *Begin with a border print and pull fabrics from your stash to match. This will tie the scraps together into a cohesive mixture when the project is complete.*

• *To use scraps in strip piecing, pull strips from your stash and join the strips randomly on the short ends to make 42"-long strips.*

• *Binding was done the same way—a minimum of 120" of 2¼"-wide strips are needed. These should be seamed diagonally as shown in Figure 10.*

**Figure 10**

• *By using consistent color placement of the scrap green (E) and navy (D) triangles, a secondary design was achieved. Even though the shades of green and navy are slightly different, because there was a distinct color change, the design still stands out.*

# Autumn Stars

Design by JULIE WEAVER

## Grace your table with this star-design runner in autumn colors, or change the colors to match your kitchen.

### Project Specifications

Skill Level: Intermediate
Runner Size: Approximately
 47" x 20"
Block Size: 8" x 8"
Number of Blocks: 3

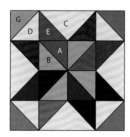

**Autumn Star**
8" x 8" Block
Make 3

### Completing the Blocks

**Step 1.** Mark a diagonal line from corner to corner on each B, D, E and F square.

**Step 2.** Referring to Figure 1, place E on C and stitch on the marked line; trim seam to ¼" and press E to the right side.

**Figure 1**

**Step 3.** Repeat Step 2 with F on the remaining end of C to complete a C-E-F unit as shown in Figure 2.

| FABRIC Measurements based on 42" usable fabric width. | #STRIPS & PIECES | CUT | #PIECES | SUBCUT |
|---|---|---|---|---|
| Assorted brown scraps | 6 | 2⅞" A squares | | |
| | 12 | 2½" E squares | | |
| | 20 | 2" x 2½" N rectangles | | |
| Assorted gold scraps | 6 | 2⅞" B squares | | |
| | 20 | 2" x 2½" N rectangles | | |
| Assorted green scraps | 6 | 2⅞" G squares | | |
| | 10 | 1½" H squares | | |
| | 20 | 2" x 2½" N rectangles | | |
| Assorted red scraps | 12 | 2½" F squares | | |
| | 20 | 2" x 2½" N rectangles | | |
| ½ yard tan tonal | 1 | 4½" x 42" | 12 | 2½" C rectangles |
| | 1 | 2⅞" x 42" | 6 | 2⅞" D squares |
| | 3 | 1" x 42" | 2 | 28" K strips |
| | | | 2 | 14" M strips |
| | | | 2 | 13" L strips |
| ½ yard tan floral tonal | 1 | 14" square | | Cut on both diagonals to make 4 J triangles |
| ½ yard brown mottled | 1 | 1½" x 42" | 12 | 8½" I strips |
| | 4 | 2¼" x 42" binding | | |
| Backing | | 52" x 25" | | |

### SUPPLIES

- Batting 53" x 24"
- All-purpose thread to match fabrics
- Quilting thread
- Basic sewing tools and supplies

**Figure 2**

**Step 4.** Repeat Steps 2 and 3 to complete 12 C-E-F units.

**Step 5.** Place an A square right sides together with a B square;

stitch ¼" on each side of the marked line as shown in Figure 3.

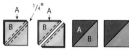

**Figure 3**

**Step 6.** Cut apart on the marked line to complete two A-B units.

**Step 7.** Repeat Steps 5 and 6 with the remaining A and B squares to make 12 A-B units and with the D and G squares to complete 12 D-G units.

**Step 8.** To complete one Autumn Star block, join two A-B units as shown in Figure 4; press seam to one side. Repeat to make two joined units.

**Figure 4**      **Figure 5**

**Step 9.** Join the two joined A-B units to complete the block center as shown in Figure 5; press seam to one side.

**Step 10.** Sew a C-E-F unit to opposite sides of the block center as shown in Figure 6; press seams toward the C-E-F units.

**Figure 6**

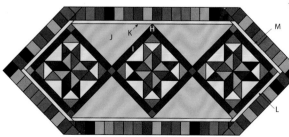

**Autumn Stars Runner**
Placement Diagram Approximately 47" x 20"

**Step 11.** Sew a D-G unit to each end of two C-E-F units to make two side rows as shown in Figure 7; press seams toward the C-E-F units.

**Figure 7**

**Step 12.** Sew a side row to opposite sides of the center row referring to the block drawing to complete one Autumn Star block; press seams toward the side rows.

**Step 13.** Repeat Steps 8–12 to complete three Autumn Star blocks.

## Completing the Runner

**Step 1.** Sew an I strip to opposite sides of each Autumn Star block; press seams toward I strips.

**Step 2.** Arrange and join the bordered blocks with the remaining I strips, H squares and J triangles in diagonal rows as shown in Figure 8.

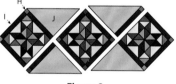

**Figure 8**

**Step 3.** Join the rows to complete the pieced center; press seams in one direction.

**Step 4.** Center and sew a K strip to opposite long sides of the pieced center; press seams toward K.

**Step 5.** Trim K using a straightedge referring to Figure 9.

**Step 6.** Add L strips, press and trim as in Step 5 as shown in Figure 10. Repeat with M strips to complete the L/M borders.

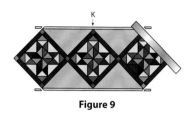

**Figure 9**

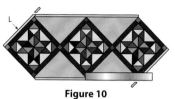

**Figure 10**

**Step 7.** Join 18 N rectangles on the long sides to make an N strip; press seams in one direction. Repeat to make two N strips.

**Step 8.** Center and sew an N strip to the K sides of the pieced center; press seams toward the N strips. Trim excess N strip as in Step 5 and referring to Figure 11.

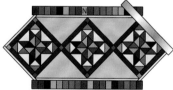

**Figure 11**

**Step 9.** Repeat Steps 7 and 8 with 10 N rectangles and sew to the L sides of the pieced center, matching at one square end as shown in Figure 12.

**Figure 12**

**Step 10.** Repeat Step 9 with 11 N rectangles on the M sides of the pieced center to complete the pieced top.

**Step 11.** Finish the runner referring to the Finishing Instructions on page 168. ◆

# Stars in the Crossroads

Design by SANDRA L. HATCH

## Make a pretty runner using assorted coordinating scraps.

### Project Specifications

Skill Level: Beginner
Runner Size: 44" x 18"
Block Size: 9" x 9"
Number of Blocks: 3

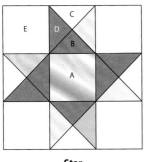

**Star**
9" x 9" Block
Make 3

### Completing the Block

**Step 1.** Sew D to B and D to C to make 12 each B-D and C-D units as shown in Figure 1; press seams toward D in each unit.

Make 12   Make 12

**Figure 1**

**Step 2.** Join one each B-D and C-D unit to complete side units as shown in Figure 2; repeat to make 12 side units.

**Figure 2**

| FABRIC<br>Measurements based on 42" usable fabric width. | #STRIPS & PIECES | CUT | #PIECES | SUBCUT |
|---|---|---|---|---|
| Scraps coordinating green, cream and rose prints and tonals | 120<br>6 | 1½" I squares<br>4¼" squares | | Cut on both diagonals to make 24 D triangles |
| ⅓ yard cream tonal | 1 | 4¼" x 42" | 3 | 4¼" squares; cut on both diagonals to make 12 C triangles |
| | 1 | 3½" x 42" | 12 | 3½" E squares |
| ⅝ yard rose tonal | 1 | 4¼" x 42" | 3 | 4¼" squares; cut on both diagonals to make 12 B triangles |
| | | | 8 | 1½" J squares |
| | | | 12 | 2" H squares |
| ¾ yard cream/pink print | 4 | 2¼" x 42" binding | | |
| | 1 | 12½" x 42" | 6 | 2" G strips |
| | | | 6 | 2" x 9½" F strips |
| | | | 3 | 3½" A squares |
| | 1 | 2½" x 42" | 2 | 2½" x 18½" L strips |
| | 2 | 2½" x 40½" K | | |
| Backing | | 50" x 24" | | |

### SUPPLIES

- Batting 50" x 24"
- All-purpose thread to match fabrics
- Quilting thread
- Basic sewing tools and supplies

**Step 3.** To complete one block, sew a side unit to opposite sides of A to make the center row as shown in Figure 3; press seams toward A.

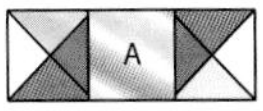

**Figure 3**

**Step 4.** Sew E to opposite sides of a side unit to make the top row as shown in Figure 4; press

seams toward E. Repeat to make the bottom row.

**Figure 4**

**Step 5.** Sew the center row between the top and bottom rows to complete the block referring to the block drawing; press seams away from the center row.

**Step 6.** Repeat Steps 3–5 to complete three blocks.

### Completing the Runner

**Step 1.** Sew an F strip to opposite sides of each pieced block; press seams toward F. Repeat with G strips on the top and bottom of each pieced block.

**Step 2.** Mark a diagonal line from corner to corner on the H squares.

**Step 3.** Pin and stitch an H square to the ends of each G strip and stitch on the marked lines as shown in Figure 5.

**Figure 5**

**Step 4.** Trim seams to ¼" and press H pieces to the right side to complete the block units as shown in Figure 6.

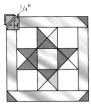

**Figure 6**

**Step 5.** Join 12 I squares to make an I strip; press seams in one direction. Repeat to make 10 I strips.

**Step 6.** Join three blocks with four I strips to complete the pieced center; press seams away from the I strips.

**Step 7.** Join three I strips with four J squares to make an I-J strip; press seams toward J squares. Repeat to make two I-J strips.

**Step 8.** Sew an I-J strip to opposite long sides of the pieced center; press seams away from the I-J strips.

**Step 9.** Sew the K strips to opposite long sides and L strips to the short sides of the pieced center; press seams toward K and L strips.

**Step 10.** Finish the quilt referring to the Finishing Instructions on page 168. ◆

**Stars in the Crossroads**
Placement Diagram 44" x 18"

*TIP*

*Some patterns are suitable for scrap quilts when only light and dark fabrics are needed. Sort through your scraps and select just the light and dark scraps; set aside the medium colors for another project.*

# Tropical Fish Mats

Designs by CONNIE RAND

## Use your brightest scraps to add a tropical look to your table setting.

### Project Specifications

Skill Level: Beginner
Mat 1 Size: 18" x 12"
Mat 2 Size: 24" x 12"

### Completing Mat 1

**Step 1.** Mark a diagonal line from corner to corner on the wrong side of each B and C square.

**Step 2.** Place a B square right sides together on opposite corners of A as shown in Figure 1; stitch on the marked line and trim seam allowance to ¼", again referring to Figure 1. Press B to the right side. Repeat on the remaining corners of A.

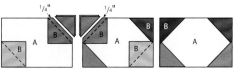

**Figure 1**

**Step 3.** Repeat Step 2 with C squares on the B corners as shown in Figure 2.

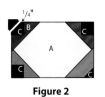

**Figure 2**

**Step 4.** Trace eye shapes onto the paper side of the fusible

| FABRIC Measurements based on 42" usable fabric width. | #STRIPS & PIECES | CUT | #PIECES | SUBCUT |
|---|---|---|---|---|
| Assorted bright-colored scraps and yellow | 4 | 6½" B squares | | |
| | 8 | 1½" x 12½" G strips | | |
| | 3 | 3" squares | | Cut in half on 1 diagonal to make 6 D triangles |
| | | Appliqué pieces as per pattern | | |
| ½ yard light blue wave print | 1 | 18½" x 12½" A piece | | |
| ¾ yard black solid | 1 | 12½" x 42" | 1 | 12½" E square |
| | | | 1 | 9⅜" square; cut in half on 1 diagonal to make 2 F triangles |
| | | | 4 | 2½" C squares |
| | 4 | 2¼" x 42" binding | | |
| Backing | 1 | 20" x 14" | | |
| | 1 | 26" x 14" | | |

### SUPPLIES

- Batting 20" x 14" and 26" x 14"
- All-purpose thread to match fabrics
- Silver and gold metallic thread
- Basting spray
- Fine-point permanent black marker
- Scraps fusible web
- Basic sewing tools and supplies and water-erasable marker

web; cut out shapes, leaving a margin around each one. Remove paper backing; set aside two eye shapes for Tropical Fish Place Mat 2. Center and fuse an eye on each C triangle referring to the Placement Diagram for positioning. Mark a dot in the center of each eye using the permanent black marker.

**Step 5.** Mark a diagonal 1" grid across the A area using a water-erasable marker.

**Step 6.** Sandwich batting between the completed top and prepared backing piece;

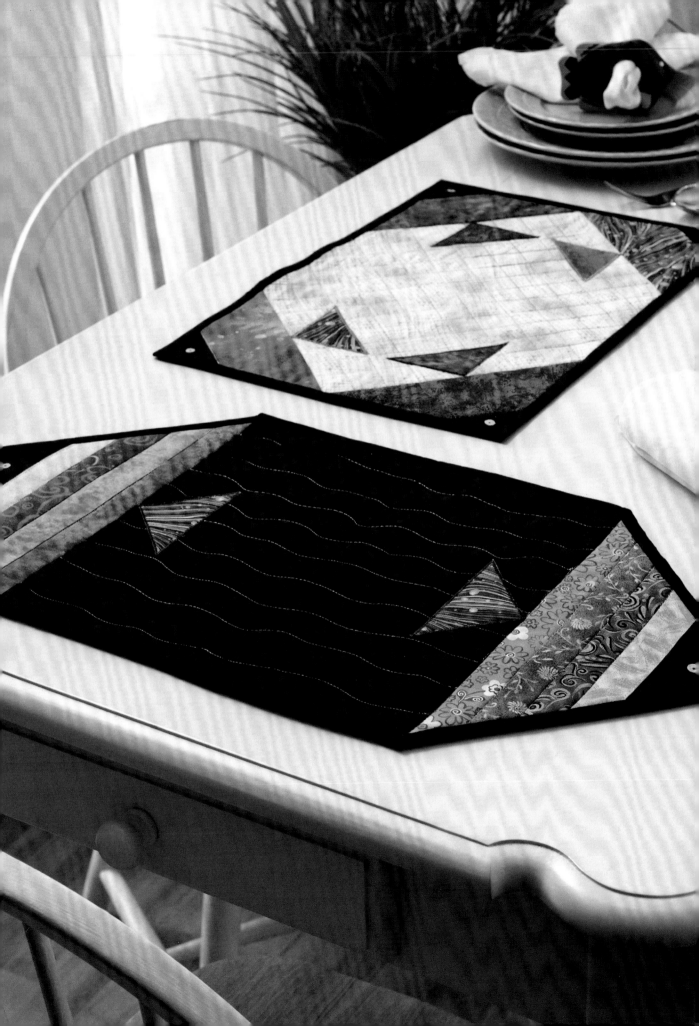

machine-quilt on the marked grid lines and in the ditch of seams.

**Step 7.** Spray-baste each D triangle on A at the center of each B corner to make tails referring to the Placement Diagram.

**Step 8.** Using thread to match D triangles and a narrow satin stitch, machine-stitch around edges of each D triangle.

**Step 9.** Bind edges referring to the Finishing Instructions on page 168 to finish.

### Completing Mat 2

**Step 1.** Place a G strip right side up on the long side of one F triangle. Place another G strip right sides together with the first strip and stitch as shown in Figure 3.

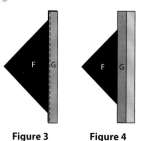

**Figure 3**        **Figure 4**

**Step 2.** Flip and press the second strip as shown in Figure 4. Continue with two more G strips.

**Step 3.** Turn under ¼" on the raw edge of the last strip and topstitch in place as shown in Figure 5 to complete one F-G unit.

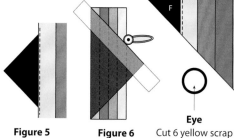

**Figure 5**        **Figure 6**

**Eye**
Cut 6 yellow scrap

**Step 4.** Repeat Steps 1–3 to make two F-G units.

**Step 5.** Turn the F-G units to the wrong side and trim strips even with edges of F referring to Figure 6.

**Step 6.** Center and sew the F-G units to E referring to the Placement Diagram.

**Step 7.** Center and fuse an eye on each F triangle referring to the Placement Diagram for positioning. Mark a dot in the center of each eye using the permanent black marker.

**Step 8.** Mark nine wavy quilting lines through the E piece using the water-erasable marker.

**Step 9.** Sandwich batting between the completed top and prepared backing piece; machine-quilt on the marked lines and in the ditch of seams.

**Step 10.** Spray-baste D triangles to E, centering at the base of the F-G units referring to the Placement Diagram to make tails.

**Step 11.** Using thread to match D triangles and a narrow satin stitch, machine-stitch around edges of each D triangle.

**Step 12.** Bind edges referring to the Finishing Instructions on page 168 to finish. ◆

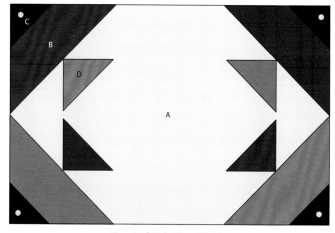

**Tropical Fish Place Mat 1**
Placement Diagram 18" x 12"

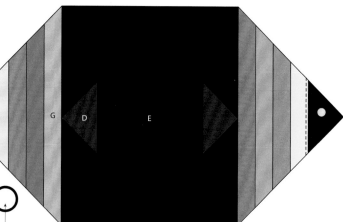

**Tropical Fish Place Mat 2**
Placement Diagram 24" x 12"

# Patchwork Growth Chart

Design by NANCY RICHOUX

## Instead of marking your wall, create a permanent record of your children's or grandchildren's growth.

### Project Specifications
Skill Level: Beginner
Chart Size: 8" x 36"

### Project Notes
The chart background can be made from five coordinating fabrics as shown in the model or from up to 34 different fabric scraps from your stash. Choose a contrasting border fabric that frames the piece. Select a yellow, white or other very light solid color for the name and height strips; it should have good contrast with the fabrics in the background.

### Completing the Chart
**Step 1.** Select two C pieces; join along the 3½" sides to make a C unit as shown in Figure 1; press seam to one side. Repeat to make eight C units.

**Step 2.** Arrange and join the C units with A and B rectangles as shown in Figure 2 to make two different long strips; press seams

**Figure 1**

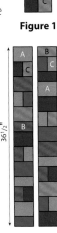

36½"

**Figure 2**

| FABRIC — Measurements based on 42" usable fabric width. | #STRIPS & PIECES | CUT |
|---|---|---|
| 16 assorted mottled scraps | 12 | 3½" x 4½" A rectangles total |
| | 6 | 2½" x 4½" B rectangles total |
| | 16 | 2½" x 3½" C rectangles total |
| 2—3¼" x 18" solid-color rectangles for name/height strips | | |
| 1—4" x 4" mottled square for pocket | | |
| 1—14" x 42" rectangle flannel for batting | | |
| ½ yard black mottled | 3 | 2¼" x 42" binding |
| | 2 | ¾" x 36½" D strips |
| | 2 | ¾" x 9" E strips |
| | 1 | 2½" x 8" for sleeve |
| Backing | | 14" x 42" |

### SUPPLIES
- All-purpose thread to match fabrics
- Quilting thread
- 1 (96") yellow tape measure
- ⅛ yard 18"-wide ultra-strong fusible web
- Black fine-point permanent fabric marker
- Hot-glue gun and glue sticks
- Basic sewing tools and supplies

open. Each strip should be 36½" long.

**Step 3.** Join the two long strips referring to the Placement Diagram for positioning; press seams open.

**Step 4.** Sew D strips to opposite long sides and E strips to the top and bottom of the pieced center; press seams toward D and E strips.

**Step 5.** Quilt the chart referring to the Finishing Instructions on page 168.

**Step 6.** Cut the tape measure at 23" and 61"; discard the cut ends.

**Step 7.** Referring to the Placement Diagram, match the 60" and 24" marks with the top and bottom border seams and center over the center seam. Glue a few inches in place at a time using the hot-glue gun. Trim ends even with outer edges of chart.

**Step 8.** Prepare for binding and bind edges referring to the Finishing Instructions on page 168.

**Step 9.** Turn under ¼" on all sides of the sleeve piece; topstitch to hem on short ends. Hand-stitch long edges to the top back, leaving the ends open.

**Step 10.** Cut one 3" x 17" strip fusible web; layer the 3¼" x 18" name/height strips with wrong sides together with fusible web between and iron to bond the layers together. Trim to 2¾" x 16". Cut into ¼" x 2¾" strips.

***Note:*** *The strip should yield 60 name strips.*

**Step 11.** Using scissors and a paper template made from pattern given, cut a point on one end of each name/height strip.

**Step 12.** Using the black fine-point marker, write name, height and date on a strip. Attach the strip to the chart with the arrow pointing to the appropriate measurement on the chart using a few dots of hot glue.

**Step 13.** Press under ¼" on three sides of the pocket square; press under ½" on the fourth side. Cut a ⅜" x 3½" strip fusible web; place under the ½" pressed area and fuse to hem.

**Step 14.** Hand-stitch the pocket in the center of the lower back, leaving fused, hemmed edge open. Place a

supply of name/height strips in the pocket for later use.

**Step 15.** Hang the chart at the correct height when measuring child for accurate measurements. ◆

> **Name/Height Strip**

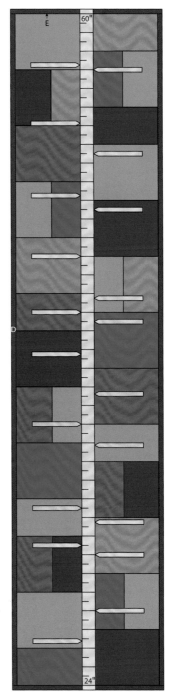

**Patchwork Growth Chart**
Placement Diagram 8" x 36"

Pocket for name/height strips on lower back.

# Triangle Illusions

Design by CONNIE KAUFFMAN

## Complementary colors like the blue and yellow scraps used in this runner are perfect fabric combinations.

### Project Specifications
Skill Level: Beginner
Runner Size: 36" x 18"

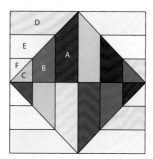

**Triangle Illusions**
9" x 9" Block
Make 3

| FABRIC<br>Measurements based on 42"<br>usable fabric width. | #STRIPS &<br>PIECES | CUT |
|---|---|---|
| Assorted blue scraps | 28 | 2" x 6" A |
| | 28 | 2" x 4½" B |
| | 28 | 3" x 3" C |
| Assorted yellow scraps | 12 | 2" x 6" D |
| | 12 | 2" x 4½" E |
| | 12 | 3" x 3" F |
| Backing | | 42" x 24" |

### SUPPLIES
- Batting 42" x 24"
- All-purpose thread to match fabrics
- Quilting thread
- Paper
- Basic sewing tools and supplies

### Completing the Units
**Step 1.** Set machine to a small stitch length to make removal of paper easier.

**Step 2.** Prepare copies of full-size paper-piecing patterns.

**Step 3.** To complete one unit, select one each A, B and C piece.

**Step 4.** Place piece A right side up on the unmarked side of the paper, covering the piece A section and extending ¼" into all surrounding sections. Place piece B right sides together with piece A on the A-B seam side as shown in Figure 1; turn paper over and stitch on the marked A-B line.

**Figure 1**

**Step 5.** Press B to the right side as shown in Figure 2.

**Figure 2**

**Step 6.** Repeat Steps 3–5 with C to complete one A-B-C unit; repeat to make 14 A-B-C units.

**Step 7.** Trim finished foundation along outside-edge line to complete the units.

**Step 8.** Repeat Steps 3–7 to complete 14 reverse A-B-C units and six each D-E-F and reverse D-E-F units referring to Figure 3.

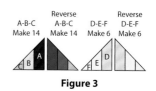

Reverse Reverse
A-B-C A-B-C D-E-F D-E-F
Make 14 Make 14 Make 6 Make 6

**Figure 3**

### Completing the Blocks
**Step 1.** Sew an A-B-C unit to a reverse D-E-F unit to make a corner unit as shown in Figure

4; repeat to make six corner units. Sew a reverse A-B-C unit to a D-E-F unit to make a reverse corner unit, again referring to Figure 4; repeat to make six reverse corner units. Press seams in one direction.

**Figure 4**

**Step 2.** Join two corner units as shown in Figure 5 to make a row; press seam in one direction. Repeat to make two rows.

**Figure 5**

**Step 3.** Join the two rows to complete one Triangle Illusions block; press seam in one direction. Repeat Steps 2 and 3 to complete three blocks.

### Completing the Quilt

**Step 1.** Join the three blocks to complete the pieced center; press seams in one direction.

**Step 2.** Join one A-B-C unit and one reverse A-B-C unit as shown in Figure 6 to make a

side unit; press seam in one direction. Repeat to make eight side units.

**Figure 6**

**Step 3.** Sew three side units to opposite long sides and one to each end of the pieced center referring to the Placement Diagram for positioning; press seams toward side units.

**Step 4.** Remove all paper.

**Step 5.** Place the batting on a flat surface with backing right side up on top; place the pieced top right sides together with the backing/batting layers and pin to hold flat.

**Step 6.** With the pieced top on the top, stitch all around ¼" from the edge of the pieced top, leaving a 6" opening on one side; trim excess batting and backing even with the edges of the pieced top. Trim batting layer even closer to the seam.

**Step 7.** Turn right side out through the opening; press edges flat.

**Step 8.** Hand-stitch opening closed; topstitch ¼" from edges all around.

**Step 9.** Quilt as desired by hand or machine to finish. ◆

**Reverse Paper-Piecing Pattern**
Make 20 copies

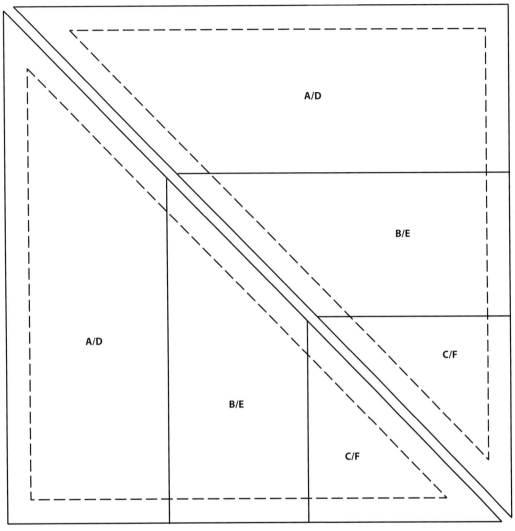

A/D

B/E

C/F

A/D

B/E

C/F

**Paper-Piecing Pattern**
Make 20 copies

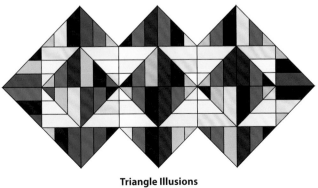

**Triangle Illusions**
Placement Diagram 36" x 18"

*TIP*

*Small scraps are wonderful for small- and medium-size paper-piecing patterns. These tiny treasures can be saved throughout the year in a box near your sewing area. When you want to paper-piece, pull out the box and have fun picking out wonderful colors in all shapes and sizes. This is a great way to recycle.*

# Love in a Tangle

Design by SANDRA L. HATCH

## A large floral is showcased in the center and wide borders of this simple quilt design.

### Project Specifications

Skill Level: Beginner
Quilt Size: 50" x 50"

### Completing the Quilt

**Step 1.** Draw a diagonal line from corner to corner on the wrong side of each E square.

**Step 2.** Place E right sides together with F; stitch ¼" on opposite sides of the marked line as shown in Figure 1. Cut apart on the marked line and press with seam toward F to make two E-F units. Repeat to make 64 E-F units.

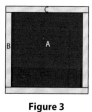

**Figure 1**

**Step 3.** Repeat Step 2 with E and I to make 16 E-I units as shown in Figure 2.

**Figure 2**

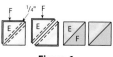

**Figure 3**

| FABRIC Measurements based on 42" usable fabric width. | #STRIPS & PIECES | CUT | #PIECES | SUBCUT |
|---|---|---|---|---|
| Assorted pink and green scraps | 32 | 2⅞" F squares | | |
| | 76 | 2½" x 6½" M pieces | | |
| | 8 | 2½" green G squares | | |
| | 2 | 4⅞" pink squares | | Cut in half on 1 diagonal to make 4 J triangles |
| 1 fat eighth pink tonal | 2 | 2⅞" x 21" | 8 | 2⅞" I squares |
| 1 fat eighth cream/pink paisley | 3 | 2½" x 21" | 20 | 2½" D squares |
| ½ yard coordinating stripe | 6 | 2¼" x 42" binding | | |
| ½ yard cream tonal | 4 | 2⅞" x 42" | 44 | 2⅞" E squares; cut 4 E squares in half on 1 diagonal to make 8 E triangles |
| | 2 | 1½" x 42" | 2 | 12½" B pieces |
| | | | 2 | 14½" C pieces |
| 1¼ yards pink/green floral | 6 | 4½" x 42" | 4 | 18½" H strips |
| | | | 4 | 30½" K strips |
| | 1 | 12½" x 42" | 1 | 12½" A square |
| | | | 4 | 6½" L squares |
| Backing | | 56" x 56" | | |

### SUPPLIES

- Batting 56" x 56"
- All-purpose thread to match fabrics
- Quilting thread
- Basic sewing tools and supplies

**Step 4.** Sew B to opposite sides of A and C to the remaining sides to complete the center unit as shown in Figure 3; press seams toward B and C.

**Step 5.** Join three E-F units to make an E-F triangle strip as

shown in Figure 4; press seams in one direction. Repeat to make four E-F triangle strips and four reverse E-F triangle strips.

Make 4    Reverse Make 4

E
F

**Figure 4**

**Step 6.** Join one E-F and reverse E-F triangle strip with D to complete a short side strip as shown on Figure 5; press seams away from D. Repeat to make four short side strips.

D

**Figure 5**

**Step 7.** Sew a short side strip to opposite sides of the center unit as shown in Figure 6; press seams toward the center unit.

D

**Figure 6**

**Step 8.** Sew D to each end of each remaining short side strip; press seams toward D. Sew a D/short side strip to the remaining sides of the center unit, again referring to Figure 6. Press seams toward the center unit.

**Step 9.** Sew D to E-I and G to E-I as shown in Figure 7; press seams toward D and G. Join the units to complete a corner unit, again referring to Figure 7; press seam in one direction. Repeat to make eight corner units.

D  E         D  E
  G            G

**Figure 7**

**Step 10.** Sew an H strip to opposite sides of the center unit; press seams toward H strips. Sew a corner unit to each end of each remaining H strip as shown in Figure 8; press seams toward H strips. Sew these strips to the remaining sides of the center unit; press seams away from the center unit.

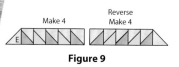

H

**Figure 8**

**Step 11.** Join five E-F units and one E triangle to make a long E-F unit as shown in Figure 9; press seams in one direction. Repeat to make four long E-F units and four long reverse E-F units.

Make 4    Reverse Make 4

E

**Figure 9**

**Step 12.** Join one each long E-F and long reverse E-F units with D to make a long side strip as shown in Figure 10; press seams toward D. Repeat to make four long side strips.

E                    D

**Figure 10**

**Step 13.** Sew a long side strip to each side of the center unit as shown in Figure 11; press seams away from the long side strips.

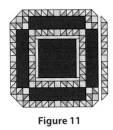

**Figure 11**

**Step 14.** Sew J to each corner; press seams toward J.

**Step 15.** Sew K to opposite sides of the center unit; press seams toward K.

**Step 16.** Sew a corner unit to each end of each remaining K strip as shown in Figure 12; press seams toward K. Sew these strips to the remaining sides of the center unit referring to the Placement Diagram for positioning. Press seams away from the center unit.

**Figure 12**

**Step 17.** Join 19 M pieces on the long sides to make a side strip; press seams in one direction. Repeat to make four side strips.

**Step 18.** Sew a side strip to opposite sides of the center unit; press seams toward side strips. Sew L to each end of each remaining side strip; press seams away from L. Sew these strips to the remaining sides of the center unit to complete the pieced top; press seams toward strips.

**Step 19.** Finish the quilt referring to the Finishing Instructions on page 168. ◆

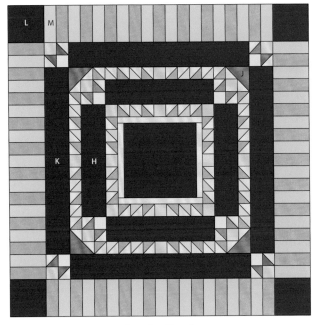

**Love in a Tangle**
Placement Diagram 50" x 50"

*TIP*

*Use scraps to try out new designs without cutting new fabrics. Save these test samples for sampler-type quilts or projects.*

# Flowers in Bloom Tea Cozy

Design by CHRIS MALONE

Serve up a warm cup of tea from a pot covered with this elegant tea cozy.

## Project Specifications
Skill Level: Advanced
Cozy Size: 13½" x 10½"

## Completing the 3-D Flowers

**Step 1.** To make each flower, fold a rose batik strip in half wrong sides together along the length; press.

**Step 2.** Align the straight edge of the U-stitch pattern on the folded edge ½" from one end as shown in Figure 1. Draw around the pattern with the air-soluble marker and move the pattern to make the next marking, leaving about ⅛" between shapes. Continue to draw pattern until five petals are traced onto the fabric with ½" left at each end; trim any excess.

| FABRIC<br>Measurements based on 42" usable fabric width. | #STRIPS & PIECES | CUT |
|---|---|---|
| Scrap gold batik | 3 | 2¼"-diameter circles |
| Fat quarter green batik | 1 | 1¼" x 20" bias strip for stem |
| Fat quarter rose batik | 3 | 3½" x 21" flower strips |
| 1 yard tan check | | Cozy pieces as per instructions |

## SUPPLIES

- 2 batting rectangles 11" x 14"
- Scrap fleece
- All-purpose thread to match fabrics
- Quilting thread
- 1 yard dark green ³⁄₁₆" piping
- 1 yard dark green single-fold bias tape for binding
- 3 (⅞") shank buttons (any color) or covered-button kits
- 11" x 14" sheet paper
- Dinner plate for pattern
- Air-soluble marker
- Fabric glue
- Zipper foot
- Basic sewing tools and supplies

**Figure 1**

**Step 3.** Thread needle with a doubled length of matching thread; hand-sew gathering stitches directly onto the pattern lines through both

layers of fabric. To move from one petal to the next, go over the edge and back into the next section as shown in Figure 2.

**Figure 2**

**Step 4.** As each petal is stitched, pull on thread to gather tightly and form petal shape. When all five petals are sewn and gathered, knot thread securely, but do not clip.

**Step 5.** Take a stitch into the edge of the first petal and pull ends together to form a flower

as shown in Figure 3; knot and clip thread. Use fingers to shape petal as needed.

**Figure 3**

**Step 6.** To cover button, hand-gather around each gold batik fabric circle ⅛" from edge; do not clip thread. Place the rounded side of a shank button on the wrong side of one fabric circle and pull thread to gather fabric around the button ; knot thread to secure. Repeat for all buttons. **Note:** *If using covered-button kits, follow directions on package to apply gold batik fabric to buttons.*

**Step 7.** Glue a covered button to each flower center, pushing shank down through the center hole to finish.

## Completing the Tea Cozy

**Step 1.** Fold the green batik bias strip in half with wrong sides together along the length; sew long edges together ¼" from raw edge. Trim seam to ⅛"; refold the strip, centering the seam on the back side as shown in Figure 4; press seam open.

**Figure 4**

**Step 2.** Trace the leaf pattern five times on the wrong side of the remaining green batik, reversing the pattern twice. Fold the fabric in half, right sides together with the traced pattern on top and pin to the fleece.

**Step 3.** Sew all around on the pattern lines; cut out each leaf shape ⅛" from the stitched seam; trim the top and clip curves.

**Step 4.** Cut a slit through one layer only of the fabric of each leaf shape and turn right side out through the slits; press well and slipstitch the opening closed.

**Step 5.** Machine-stitch through the center of each leaf shape.

## Completing the Leaves & Bias Stems

**Step 1.** Fold the 11" x 14" paper rectangle in half to make an 11" x 7" double layer.

**Step 2.** Use a dinner plate as a pattern to gently round the top corner opposite the folded edge as shown in Figure 5.

**Figure 5**

**Step 3.** Use the paper pattern to cut four cozy pieces from the tan check for front, back and lining.

**Step 4.** Place one cozy lining wrong side up with batting on top; smooth the cozy front in place with right side up.

**Step 5.** Mark a 2" diagonal grid for quilting on the cozy front with the air-soluble marker. Pin and baste the layers together. Prepare cozy back in the same manner.

**Step 6.** Quilt on the marked lines by hand or machine.

**Step 7.** With raw edges even, pin piping to the curved sides and top of the cozy front; attach zipper foot to sewing

machine and machine-baste close to piping cord as shown in Figure 6.

**Figure 6**

**Step 8.** Pin the cozy front and back pieces with right sides together and raw edges even; stitch the layers together, positioning the stitches just inside the machine-basting line for piping. Finish seam with a close zigzag stitch or serger.

**Step 9.** Unfold the bias binding; beginning in the center of the back bottom raw edge of the cozy, pin the binding all around. When you reach the end, trim excess if needed and fold the short end under ¼" to overlap the beginning tape as shown in Figure 7; stitch in the fold line.

**Figure 7**

**Step 10.** Wrap the bias tape over the raw edge to inside of the cozy and slipstitch in place.

**Step 11.** Transfer the stem lines to the cozy front using the air-soluble marker.

**Step 12.** Pin prepared bias stem on the lines, cutting off two short sections for stems that are branching off as shown on pattern; hand-stitch stems to cozy front.

**Step 13.** Referring to the Placement Diagram and project photo, arrange flowers and leaves along the appliquéd stems; apply fabric glue to the center back of each flower and press in place.

**Step 14.** Apply a line of fabric glue to the back of each leaf along the stitched vein line; press in place to finish. ◆

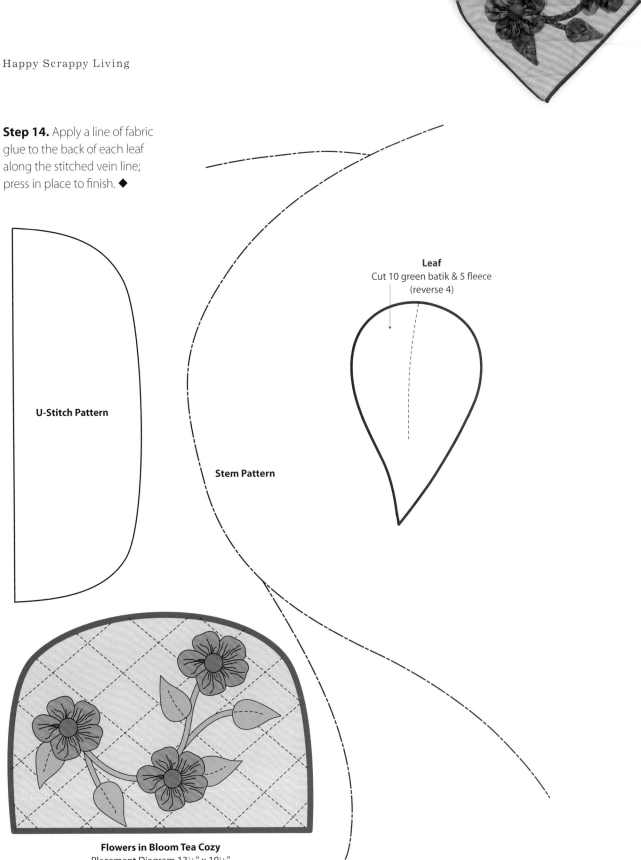

**U-Stitch Pattern**

**Stem Pattern**

**Leaf**
Cut 10 green batik & 5 fleece
(reverse 4)

**Flowers in Bloom Tea Cozy**
Placement Diagram 13¹/₂" x 10¹/₂"

# Patchwork Bags

Nothing tells others that you are a quilter like carrying a bag or tote that is created out of scraps. To show you how versatile scrappy bags can be, we've included designs for a variety of occasions. Stitch a patchwork tote to take to the beach, create an elegant wedding gift bag or make a small bag to use when you need to carry sewing supplies with you. For even more variety, use scraps of denim to make a stylish carry-every-day purse.

# Scrappy Sewing Pod

Designs by JODI G. WARNER

## Two easy variations use the same construction methods in these scrappy sewing pods.

### Project Specifications
Skill Level: Beginner
Pod Size: 8" x 3" x 3"

### Completing Sewing Pod A

**Step 1.** Join one each X, Z and Y along the 4¼" edges as shown in Figure 1; press seams in one direction. Repeat to make three X-Z-Y units.

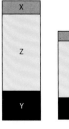

| Figure 1 | Figure 2 |
|----------|----------|

**Step 2.** Join the X-Z-Y units to complete the sewing pod body as shown in Figure 2; press seams open.

**Step 3.** Layer the sewing pod body with batting and lining and machine-quilt as desired; trim to 11½" x 11".

**Step 4.** Stitch ⅛" from edge all around to secure.

**Step 5.** Position one edge of zipper tape with edge of body piece approximately ³⁄₁₆" from zipper teeth; topstitch in place as shown in Figure 3.

| FABRIC<br>Measurements based<br>on 42" usable fabric width. | #STRIPS & PIECES | CUT |
|---|---|---|
| Assorted bright-colored scraps | 3 | 4¼" x 2¼" X |
| | 3 | 4¼" x 3¼" Y |
| | 3 | 4¼" x 7¾" Z |
| | 1 | 1½" x 11" Q |
| | 1 | 4½" x 11" R |
| | 3 | 4" x 4" S |
| | 4 | 1½" x 11" T |
| | 2 | 1½" x 7" U |
| | 4 | 1½" x 8" binding |
| Backing | 2 | 12" x 12" |

#### SUPPLIES

- 2 pieces batting 12" x 12"
- All-purpose thread to match fabrics
- Quilting thread
- 2 (14") zippers
- Basic sewing tools and supplies

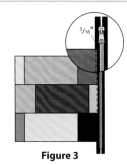

**Figure 3**

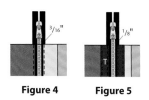

| Figure 4 | Figure 5 |
|----------|----------|

**Step 6.** Mark edges of body piece on opposite ends of zipper; open the zipper. Position and topstitch remaining edge of zipper tape in place between marks on the opposite edge of the sewing pod body and close zipper as shown in Figure 4.

**Step 7.** Fold under ⅜" on both long edges of each T band to form a ¾" finished strip; press.

**Step 8.** Topstitch a T band in place ⅛" from zipper teeth on each side of the zipper, covering the stitching for zipper as shown in Figure 5.

**Step 9.** Repeat stitching on the opposite side of T to complete

zipper cover, again referring to Figure 5.

**Step 10.** Move zipper slide midway into body; align open edges of the zipper and baste across both ends. Cut off excess zipper ends as shown in Figure 6.

**Figure 6**

**Step 11.** Fold long raw edges of U loop strip to the center, and then fold again so folded edges align as shown in Figure 7; stitch close to both edges to hold.

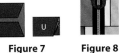

**Figure 7**        **Figure 8**

**Step 12.** Cut one U loop strip into two 3½" pieces.

**Step 13.** Place raw ends over ends of zipper as shown in Figure 8; baste across ends to secure.

**Step 14.** Turn inside out; align edges on one end of bag and form a pleat with edges even with zipper edges as shown in Figure 9; stitch across folded

edge, securing stitches at the beginning and end of seam and over the trimmed zipper end. Repeat on remaining end of bag.

**Figure 9**

**Step 15.** Fold the 1½" x 8" binding strip in half wrong sides together along length to prepare a double-fold strip. Enclose the stitched ends with the strip and stitch in place as shown in Figure 10; turn right side out to finish.

**Figure 10**

## Completing Sewing Pod B

**Step 1.** Join the long and short O pieces with P and PR to make the O-P side of the bag top as shown in Figure 11; press seams in one direction.

**Figure 11**

**Step 2.** Join three S squares to complete the S side of

the bag top; press seams in one direction.

**Step 3.** Join the S and O-P sides with Q and R strips to complete the Sewing Pod B top as shown in Figure 12; press seams toward R.

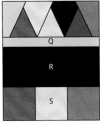

**Figure 12**

**Step 4.** Complete the sewing pod referring to Steps 3–15 of Completing Sewing Pod A to complete Sewing Pod B. ◆

*Templates are on page 173*

**Sewing Pod A**
Placement Diagram 8" x 3" x 3"

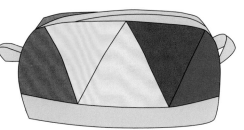

**Sewing Pod B**
Placement Diagram 8" x 3" x 3"

# Starfish Beach Tote

Design by BARBARA CLAYTON

## Use a patchwork block as the front side of a sturdy canvas beach tote.

### Project Specifications
Skill Level: Advanced
Tote Size: 15½" x 15½" x 4"

**Swirling Stars**
13½" x 13½" Block
Make 1

| FABRIC Measurements based on 42" usable fabric width. | #STRIPS & PIECES | CUT |
|---|---|---|
| Scrap brown mottled | | Appliqué pieces as per pattern |
| Scraps brown, cream, pink and tan | 2 | 5⅜" C squares each color |
| | 1 | 5" A square cream only |
| | 4 | 2¾" B squares pink only |
| 1¼ yards cream canvas | 2 | 1½" x 14" D strips |
| | 2 | 1½" x 16" E strips |
| | 4 | 16" backing and lining squares |
| | 6 | 4½" x 16½" F side strips |
| | 2 | 6" x 19" handle strips |
| | 1 | 1¾" x 39½" facing strip |

### SUPPLIES

- 16" x 16" square low-loft batting
- All-purpose thread to match fabrics
- Quilting thread
- Clear nylon thread

- Water-soluble marker
- Freezer paper
- Water-soluble glue stick
- Sponge or cloth
- Basic sewing tools and supplies

### Completing the Swirling Stars Block

**Step 1.** Draw a diagonal line from corner on the wrong side of each B and C square.

**Step 2.** Place a pink C square right sides together with a cream C square and stitch ¼" on each side of the marked line as shown in Figure 1.

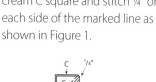

**Figure 1**

**Step 3.** Cut stitched square apart on the marked line and press seams toward darker fabric to make two C units as shown in Figure 2; repeat to

make four each pink/cream C units and brown/tan C units, again referring to Figure 2.

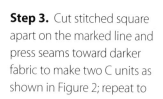

**Figure 2**

**Step 4.** Place a marked B square on opposite corners of A and stitch on the marked line as

shown in Figure 3; trim seam to ¼" and press B to the right side, again referring to Figure 3.

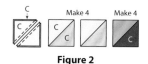
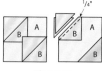

**Figure 3**

**Step 5.** Repeat Step 4 on the remaining sides of A to

complete the A-B unit as shown in Figure 4.

**Figure 4**

**Step 6.** Join two pink/cream C units with one brown/tan C unit to complete a C row as shown in Figure 5; press seams toward the center unit. Repeat to make two C rows.

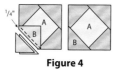

**Figure 5**

**Step 7.** Sew a brown/tan C unit to opposite sides of the A-B unit to complete the center row referring to Figure 6; press seams toward the C units.

**Figure 6**

**Step 8.** Sew a C row to opposite sides of the center row referring to the block drawing to complete the background for the Swirling Star block; press seams in one direction.

**Step 9.** Trace the starfish shape onto the paper side of the freezer paper. Layer paper to cut several paper shapes at once; cut five paper shapes.

**Step 10.** Press the waxy side of the freezer-paper shapes to the wrong side of the brown mottled scrap.

**Step 11.** Cut around each shape, leaving a ¼" turn-under seam allowance all around; clip curves, points and indentations almost to the paper pattern.

**Step 12.** Using a glue stick, glue the ¼" excess fabric over

the edge and to the back of the freezer paper all around.

**Step 13.** Referring to the block drawing, center and pin a starfish on the four corner C units and the center A-B unit.

**Step 14.** Stitch around the outside edge of each starfish shape using a narrow machine blind hemstitch and clear nylon thread.

**Step 15.** Turn the block to the back side and make a slit behind each starfish shape. Trim away the fabric to ¼" from the edge of each shape; use a sponge or wet cloth to wet the back of each shape. Tear away the freezer paper; let dry and press.

**Step 16.** Sew D strips to opposite sides and E strips to the remaining sides of the pieced block; press seams toward D and E strips.

**Step 17.** Referring to Figure 7, mark straight lines ¾" apart on all tan C triangles starting ¾" from the outside edge of each triangle; mark diagonal lines ¾" apart on the brown C triangles starting ¾" from the diagonal seam.

**Figure 7**

**Step 18.** Sandwich the batting between the finished block and a 16" canvas square; machine-quilt in the ditch of seams with clear nylon thread and hand-quilt on marked lines and ¼" from starfish shapes with quilting thread. Moisten to remove marker lines.

## Completing the Tote

**Step 1.** Join three F strips on short ends and trim to make a 48½"-long strip; repeat to make two long F strips. Press seams toward the center strips.

**Step 2.** Pin one F strip right sides together with the quilted block and stitch as shown in Figure 8, clipping corners as you go; press seams toward F.

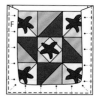

**Figure 8**

**Step 3.** Sew a 16" canvas square to the remaining side of the strip to complete the bag shell; press seams toward F. Turn right side out.

**Step 4.** Sew the other long F strip to three sides of a 16" canvas square, clipping the corners again and sewing the remaining 16" canvas square to the other side of the strip to make lining; press seams toward F.

**Step 5.** Topstitch close to stitched seam on the F pieces of both the bag and lining sections as shown in Figure 9.

**Figure 9**

**Step 6.** Insert the lining inside the top with wrong sides together, matching F seams; pin at top edge.

**Step 7.** Stitch a scant ¼" seam from the top raw edge of the tote with a long basting stitch.

**Step 8.** Fold over both raw edges of each handle strip ¼"; press to hold.

Patchwork Bags

**Step 9.** Fold each strip along length with wrong sides together, matching folded edges; topstitch close to open folded edge to complete each handle strip as shown in Figure 10. Topstitch close to the opposite edge.

Figure 10

**Step 10.** Pin the end of a handle strip to the top edge of the tote front with raw edges aligned, starting 4" from the left seam and pinning the other handle end 4" from the right seam; stitch to tack in place. Repeat for the second handle on the tote back.

**Step 11.** Join the short ends of the facing strip with a ¼" seam allowance to make a tube; press seam open. Press under one edge ¼".

**Step 12.** Pin the raw edge of the tube to the top of the tote with right sides together and handles between the layers; stitch all around catching the handles in the seam.

**Step 13.** Fold the facing to the wrong side; press. Topstitch in place along the folded edge of the tube and close to the top edge of the tote to finish. ◆

**Starfish Beach Tote**
Placement Diagram 15½" x 15½" x 4"

**Starfish**
Cut 5 brown mottled scrap

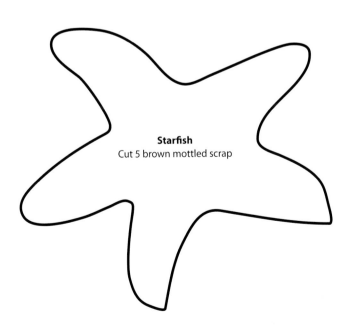

# Wedding Gift Bag

Design by SANDRA L. HATCH

## Make an heirloom gift bag for the special bride and groom.

### Project Specifications
Skill Level: Beginner
Bag Size: 17½" x 19½"

### Completing the Embroidered Strip
**Step 1.** Measure in ½" from each end of A and mark. Divide A into four equal sections and mark.

**Step 2.** Cut and pin fabric stabilizer strips to fit along the center of the A strip.

**Step 3.** Using gold metallic thread, machine-stitch a message through the center of one of the four sections marked on A. Repeat the message stitching on A to complete the embroidery as shown in Figure 1; set aside. **Note:** *If your sewing machine doesn't have alphabet embroidery patterns, transfer the message given onto A and use 2 strands gold embroidery floss and a backstitch to create the message.*

**Figure 1**

### Making Handles
**Step 1.** Fold one long edge of each B strip ¼" to the wrong side and press.

| FABRIC<br>Measurements based on 42" usable fabric width. | #STRIPS &<br>PIECES | CUT | #PIECES | SUBCUT |
|---|---|---|---|---|
| 84—3" x 3" D squares assorted white tonals | | | | |
| ⅛ yard white tonal | 1 | 3" x 42" A strip | | |
| ⅛ yard gold lamé | 2 | 1" x 42" C strips | | |
| ⅞ yard white tonal | 1 | 3" x 42"<br>Bag lining as directed in instructions | 2 | 21" B strips |

### SUPPLIES
- Batting 23" x 38" and 2 (1" x 21") strips
- All-purpose thread to match fabrics
- Quilting thread
- Gold metallic thread or embroidery floss
- 2 (2½") white satin roses
- ¼ yard fabric stabilizer
- 2 (1½" x 38") strips lightweight fusible interfacing
- 4" length ¼"-wide white satin ribbon
- 2 gold rings
- Air-soluble marker (optional)
- Press cloth
- Basic sewing tools and supplies

**Step 2.** Fold over opposite long edge of each strip 1" as shown in Figure 2 and press; fold the pressed ¼" edge over ¾" on top of the raw edge of the pressed 1" edge and press.

**Step 3.** Open the pressed edges of each strip and insert the 1"-wide batting strip, aligning batting strip with pressing lines as shown in Figure 3.

**Step 4.** Refold pressed edges over the batting, first folding over the 1" edges and overlapping with the ¾"

**Figure 2**     **Figure 3**

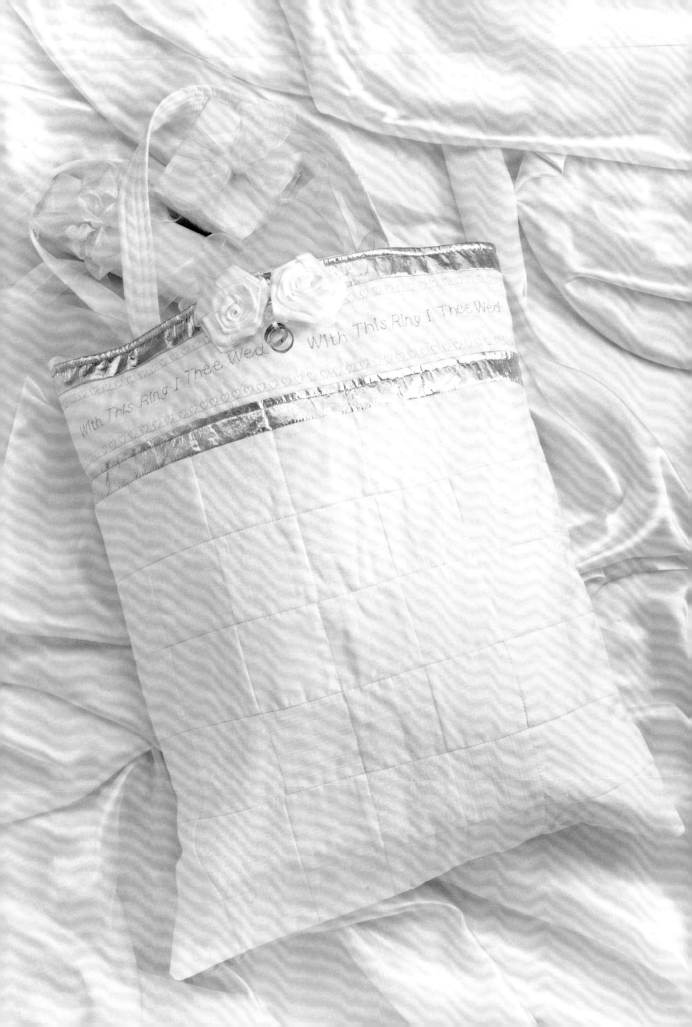

finished edge; press to make 1"-wide strips.

**Step 5.** Stitch along folded-over edge along center of strips as shown in Figure 4. Stitch ¼" from each side of the stitched line as shown in Figure 5.

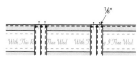

**Figure 4**

**Figure 5**

**Step 6.** Square-up ends of each strip to complete handles.

## Completing the Bag Top

**Step 1.** Randomly join 14 D squares to make a D strip; press seams in one direction. Repeat to make six D strips.

**Step 2.** Join the D strips, alternating seam allowances in rows; press seams in one direction.

**Step 3.** Iron a lightweight fusible interfacing strip to the wrong side of each C strip using a press cloth. **Note:** *Do not touch a hot iron directly on the right side of the gold lamé strips because it could disintegrate; use a press cloth.*

**Step 4.** Sew the embroidered A strip between the two C strips; using the press cloth, press seams toward the C strips.

**Step 5.** Sew the A-C strip to the top edge of the pieced D section to complete the bag top as shown in Figure 6.

**Figure 6**

**Step 6.** Center and pin the bag top right side up on the batting piece; quilt as desired. **Note:** *The sample shown was quilted in the ditch of all horizontal seams and every other vertical seam in the D section and in the ditch of seams of the A and C pieces.*

**Step 7.** When quilting is complete, trim batting edges even with the quilted top.

**Step 8.** Machine-stitch a line of a selected embroidery stitch above and below the stitched message. **Note:** *The sample used a built-in heart design and gold metallic thread.*

## Attaching Handles

**Step 1.** Fold the quilted bag top in half along the width and lay on a flat surface.

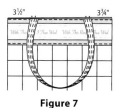

**Figure 7**

**Step 2.** Measure in 3¾" from the raw edge and pin the right side of one end of one handle to the top right side edge of the bag as shown in Figure 7. Measure in 3½" from the folded edge and pin the opposite end of the same handle right sides together with bag top edge, again referring to Figure 7. **Note:** *The right side of the handle strip is the side without the overlapped edge.*

**Step 3.** Turn folded bag top over, align and pin the second handle even with the ends of the handle pinned in Step 2 as shown in Figure 8.

**Figure 8**

**Step 4.** Machine-stitch over ends of handles several times to secure in place as shown in Figure 9.

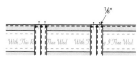

**Figure 9**

## Lining & Finishing the Bag

**Step 1.** Using the quilted bag top as a pattern, cut a lining piece from lining fabric.

**Step 2.** Place lining piece right sides together with quilted top. Stitch across top edge of bag, stitching over handle ends.

**Step 3.** Press seam toward lining and topstitch close to seam on lining to catch seam allowance in stitching side as shown in Figure 10.

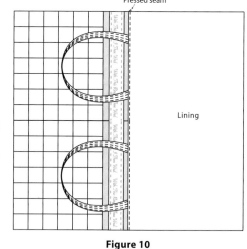

**Figure 10**

**Step 4.** Fold bag top and lining sections with right sides together as shown in Figure 11. Starting at the bag bottom corner, stitch all around bag top and lining, leaving a 6" opening in the bottom edge of the lining as shown in Figure 12.

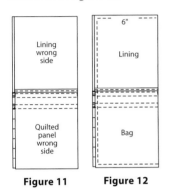

**Figure 11**          **Figure 12**

**Step 5.** Trim corners of bag top and lining and trim batting close to seam at top side edge and along bottom corners to reduce bulk.

**Step 6.** Turn right side out through opening in lining, making sure corners are completely turned.

**Step 7.** Press seam inside at lining opening edges and machine-stitch opening closed close to edges as shown in Figure 13.

**Figure 13**

**Step 8.** Before inserting lining inside bag, press side seam of bag to help make bag lie flat at sides when complete.

**Step 9.** Insert lining inside bag. Press lining to the inside at the top edge of the bag using press cloth. Insert iron inside bag and press lining flat as far inside as the iron will slide. Hold the top side of the bag and insert your hand inside the bag to the corners to be sure lining is completely inside and aligned at corners.

**Step 10.** Topstitch along top edge of bag ¼"–⅜" from edge using matching all-purpose thread.

**Step 11.** Choose another area on the bag band and machine-quilt to hold lining layer and bag top together. **Note:** *This may be in the seam of a strip or ¼" from a seam or in the center of a strip.*

**Step 12.** Hand-stitch two ribbon roses to the center of the bag front top edge.

**Step 13.** Loop the 4" white satin ribbon through the two rings; hand-stitch ends of ribbon in the center between the two white ribbon roses and tack ends of ribbon roses on top to conceal stitching to complete the bag. ◆

**Wedding Gift Bag**
Placement Diagram 17½" x 19½"

*With This Ring I Thee Wed*

**Message**

# A Denim Beauty

Design by BARBARA CLAYTON

## Turn your old jeans into a purse—one that is perfect for use when wearing your favorite blue jeans.

### Project Specifications
Skill Level: Advanced
Purse Size: 10½" x 8¼" x 4"

### Completing the Purse Front & Back
**Step 1.** Join the A, B and C denim strips in alphabetical order with right sides together along length to make a strip set; press seams in one direction. Repeat with all A, B and C strips.
**Step 2.** Subcut the A-B-C strip sets into a total of (56) 2" A-B-C units as shown in Figure 1.

**Figure 1**

**Step 3.** Arrange and join seven A-B-C units to make an X row as shown in Figure 2; press seams in one direction. Repeat to make four X rows. Repeat to make four Y rows, again referring to Figure 2.

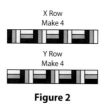

X Row
Make 4

Y Row
Make 4

**Figure 2**

**Step 4.** Join two each X and Y rows to make the pieced front section; press rows in one

| FABRIC<br>Measurements based on 42"<br>usable fabric width. | #STRIPS &<br>PIECES | CUT |
|---|---|---|
| Light (C) and medium blue (B) denim scraps | | 1"-wide strips each B and C to total 120" |
| ⅔ yard lightweight light blue denim | 2 | 4½" x 11" E |
| | 2 | 2¾" x 11" F |
| | 1 | 6" x 38" strip |
| | 1 | 4½" x 28½" D |
| 1¼ yards lightweight navy denim | | 1"-wide A strips to total 120" |
| | 1 | 1" x 22" bias stem strip |
| | 1 | 1¼" x 7" bias G strip |
| | 2 | 9" x 11" lining rectangles |
| | 1 | 4½" x 28½" D lining |
| | | Appliqué pieces as per pattern |

### SUPPLIES
- Batting 32" x 11"
- All-purpose thread to match fabrics
- Clear nylon thread
- ¼ yard heavyweight fusible stabilizer
- Fabric glue stick
- 1⅛" navy button
- 6" (¼") drapery piping
- ¼" bias bar
- 10" x 7" template plastic
- Denim machine-sewing needle
- Basic sewing tools and supplies

direction. Repeat to make the back section.
**Step 5.** Sew an F strip to the top edge of the front and back sections as shown in Figure 3.

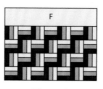

**Figure 3**

### Preparing the Appliqués
**Step 1.** Trace the heart and leaf shapes onto the cloth side of the heavyweight fusible stabilizer referring to patterns for number to cut; cut out shapes. Fuse the shapes onto the wrong side of the navy denim, leaving at least ¼" between shapes.

**Step 2.** Cut out fabric shapes, adding ¼" all around each piece for a turn-under seam allowance when cutting.

**Step 3.** Using the fabric glue stick, turn seam allowance over stabilizer shapes, clipping curves, points and indentations as necessary.

**Step 4.** Cut the 1" x 22" bias stem strip into four 5½" lengths for vines.

**Step 5.** Fold each strip in half along the length with wrong sides together; stitch a ¼" seam along the length of each strip. Trim seam to ⅛".

**Step 6.** Rotate the seam to the center back of the stitched strips; insert ¼" bias bar inside and press seams open to complete the stem pieces.

**Completing the Purse**

**Step 1.** Arrange and stitch the bias stem, leaf and heart shapes on one E rectangle and to the back F piece as shown in Figure 4 and referring to the Heart, Vine & Leaf Diagram; hand-stitch in place when satisfied with placement.

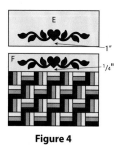

**Figure 4**

**Step 2.** Cut two 11" x 9" batting rectangles for purse front and back. Pin the pieced front and back sections to the batting with right sides up.

**Step 3.** For purse front, pin a 9" x 11" lining rectangle to the purse front with right sides

together; stitch across the top edge through all layers.

**Step 4.** Fold the lining to the back of the purse front and press the finished edge; topstitch ¼" from both the top edge and on the bottom edge of F as shown in Figure 5. Pin remainder of lining to the layered purse front to hold flat.

**Figure 5**

**Step 5.** Machine-quilt in the ditch of seams and around appliqué shapes using clear nylon thread.

**Step 6.** Fold the 7" G strip in half along length with right sides together; stitch along the long edge to make a tube as shown in Figure 6. Turn right side out.

**Figure 6**

**Step 7.** Pin a large safety pin to the end of the 6" piece of piping and insert into the tube; pull through to fill the tube, leaving ½" on each end empty to reduce bulk in seam.

**Step 8.** Fold the piping tube in half and pin ends at the center of the bottom edge of E as shown in Figure 7; baste to hold in place.

**Figure 7**

**Step 9.** Pin the appliquéd E piece right sides together with the remaining E piece; round the bottom corners as shown in Figure 8.

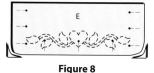

**Figure 8**

**Step 10.** Using the layered E pieces as a pattern, cut a piece of batting and pin to the layered pieces.

**Step 11.** Stitch around two ends and the bottom long side of layered pieces; turn right side out and press flat.

**Step 12.** Topstitch around the three stitched edges of the flap ¼" from edge.

**Step 13.** Machine-quilt flap as in Step 5.

**Step 14.** Center the flap pieces right sides together along the F edge of the batting/purse back; place the remaining 9" x 11" lining piece right sides together with the purse back with flap between. Stitch through all layers. Trim flap seam allowance close to seam line to reduce bulk.

**Step 15.** Fold lining to the back, stitch and machine-quilt as for purse front in Steps 4 and 5.

**Step 16.** Fold the ends of the D strips in half right sides together and stitch a 2"-long pleat 2¼" from the folded edge as shown in Figure 9. Repeat with the D lining strip.

**Figure 9**

**Step 17.** Center and flatten the pleat on the wrong side; baste across the top of each pleat; set the lining strip aside.

**Step 18.** Pin the D strip around the edges of the quilted purse front with right sides together as shown in Figure 10; stitch. Add the quilted purse back to the stitched unit to complete

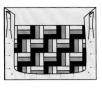

the bag shell. **Note:** *Clip strip at the bottom edge corners to allow for easing around bottom corners.*

**Figure 10**

**Step 19.** Fold over both raw edges of each handle strip ¼"; press to hold.

**Step 20.** Fold each strip along length with wrong sides together, matching folded edges; topstitch close to open folded edge to complete each handle strip as shown in Figure 11. Topstitch close to the opposite edge, again referring to Figure 11.

**Figure 11**

**Step 21.** Pin handle ends to the top inside edge of the pleated D strips at bag top and stitch across twice to secure in place.

**Step 22.** Pin the pleated ends of the D lining strip to the top edge of the purse sides with right sides together over handle ends. Stitch this seam twice to secure handles between the bag and lining.

**Step 23.** Pin the side of the lining strip to the sides and bottom of the purse, clipping at the corners; stitch the three sides. **Note:** *This is the most difficult seam because you are stitching so close to the handles. If you can't make it all the way to the handles, go as far as you can and backstitch.* Slipstitch the tight part by the handles with a double length of thread with invisible hand stitches.

**Step 24.** Fold the other edge of the D strip under ¼" and pin to the inside sides of the purse. Hand-slipstitch the lining in place along both sides.

**Step 25.** Cut the sheet of template plastic into two 10" x 3½" rectangles. Cut the four corners of each rectangle slightly round so they won't poke holes in the purse over time.

**Step 26.** Place the plastic rectangles together and wrap with the remaining quilt batting. Hand-slipstitch the batting to secure around the plastic.

**Step 27.** Insert the padded plastic into the bottom of the purse. Fold the opening in the lining over ¼" and pin to the bottom inside back of the purse; slipstitch in place, catching the batting in the stitches to keep the covered

plastic in place. Turn the purse right side out.

**Step 28.** Sew the button to the center A-B-C unit on the second row from the top on the purse front. Use a double strand of thread and place something like a matchstick under the button to sew a long shank. Stitch many times, then remove the matchstick and wind the thread around the shank and knot off close to purse.

**Step 29.** Fold the flap down over the purse front and hook the loop over the button. Slipstitch the loop together about ¾" so that the loop fits the button snugly but can still be removed easily. ◆

**A Denim Beauty**
Placement Diagram 10½" x 8¼" x 4"

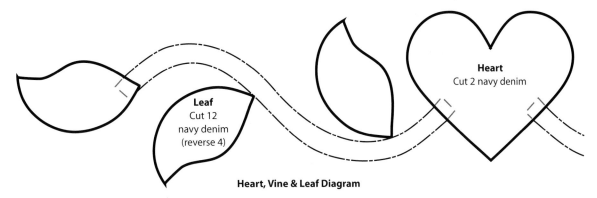

**Leaf**
Cut 12
navy denim
(reverse 4)

**Heart**
Cut 2 navy denim

**Heart, Vine & Leaf Diagram**

# Little Treasures
# Baby Quilts

Baby quilts are often the first project many quilters make. They want to make a quilt for their first baby and find that they love the whole process of quilting, from selecting fabric to quilting the top to stitching on the binding and adding a label. Years later they are still making baby quilts, only now the quilts are for the grandbabies. Babies and quilts seem to go together.

# Cute as a Bug Baby Quilt

Design by CHRIS MALONE

Bright-colored scraps and colorful appliqués make the perfect baby quilt.

## Project Specifications
Skill Level: Beginner
Quilt Size: 48" x 48"
Block Size: 6" x 6"
Number of Blocks: 49

**Strip Block**
6" x 6" Block
Make 25

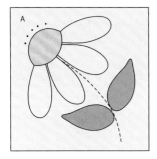

**Flower**
6" x 6" Block
Make 12
(Reverse 6)

| FABRIC<br>Measurements based on 43" usable fabric width. | #STRIPS & PIECES | CUT | #PIECES | SUBCUT |
|---|---|---|---|---|
| Assorted scraps | 75 | 2½" x 6½" B rectangles | | |
| | 4 | 3½" D squares gold | | |
| Scraps red, blue, rose, green, gold, aqua and white prints, dots and tonals | | Appliqué pieces as per patterns | | |
| ½ yard green dot | 5 | 2¼" x 43" binding | | |
| ½ yard red dot | 4 | 3½" x 42½" C | | |
| 1 yard cream tonal | 4 | 7" x 43" | 24 | 7" A squares |
| Backing | | 54" x 54" | | |

## SUPPLIES
- Batting 54" x 54"
- All-purpose thread to match fabrics
- Quilting thread
- Black, green and gold embroidery floss
- 2 yards 18"-wide fusible web
- 1½ yards fabric stabilizer
- Air-soluble pen
- Basic sewing tools and supplies

## Completing the Strip Blocks
**Step 1.** Join three B rectangles referring to the block drawing to complete one Strip Block; press seams in one direction. Repeat to make 25 blocks.

## Completing the Appliquéd Blocks
**Step 1.** Cut (24) 6 x 6" squares fabric stabilizer.
**Step 2.** Trace appliqué shapes onto the paper side of the fusible web referring to patterns

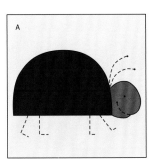

**Bug 1**
6" x 6" Block
Make 2
(Reverse 1)

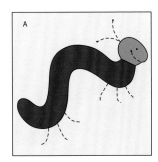

**Bug 2**
6" x 6" Block
Make 2
(Reverse 1)

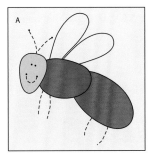

**Bug 3**
6" x 6" Block
Make 2
(Reverse 1)

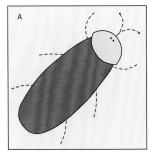

**Bug 4**
6" x 6" Block
Make 2
(Reverse 1)

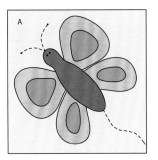

**Bug 5**
6" x 6" Block
Make 2

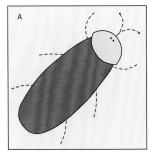

**Butterfly**
6" x 6" Block
Make 2

given for number to cut; cut out shapes leaving a margin around each one.

**Step 3.** Fuse shapes to the wrong side of fabrics as directed on patterns for color; cut out shapes on traced lines. **Note:** *Because there are many similar shaped pieces, it is helpful to label the pieces on the paper side, for example Bug 1, Bug 2, etc.*

**Step 4.** Fold A squares in quarters and crease to mark centers; arrange and fuse flower-motif pieces in numerical order on one A square referring to the pattern and project photo for positioning of pieces.

**Step 5.** Pin a fabric-stabilizer square to the wrong side of the A square.

**Step 6.** Using thread to match fabrics and a machine blanket stitch or medium-width zigzag stitch, sew around each fused shape. Remove fabric stabilizer.

**Step 7.** Transfer the stem design to the block using the air-soluble pen. Using 2 strands green embroidery floss and a stem stitch, embroider on the marked line. Embroider French knots above the flower center using 2 strands gold embroidery floss.

**Step 8.** Repeat Steps 4–7 to complete two each Flower and all bug blocks, transferring legs, antennae, smiles, butterfly trail and eyes to blocks referring to patterns. **Note:** *Reverse the design when fusing one of each bug block to create reverse blocks. Note that some pieces are symmetrical and do not require reversing.*

**Step 9.** Using 2 strands black embroidery floss, outline stitch each leg, antenna and smile and use a French knot for eyes and at the ends of each smile and antenna. Sew a running stitch for the butterfly trail.

**Completing the Quilt**

**Step 1.** Arrange the appliquéd blocks with the Strip Blocks in seven rows of seven blocks each referring to the Placement Diagram for positioning of blocks.

**Step 2.** Join blocks in rows as arranged, being careful to pin blocks in the proper position before joining; press seams toward the appliquéd blocks in each row.

**Step 3.** Join the rows as arranged to complete the pieced center; press seams in one direction.

**Step 4.** Sew a C strip to opposite sides of the pieced center; press seams toward C strips.

**Step 5.** Sew a D square to each end of each remaining C strip; press seams toward C.

**Step 6.** Sew a C-D strip to the top and bottom of the pieced center to complete the pieced top; press seams toward C-D strips.

**Step 7.** Finish the quilt referring to the Finishing Instructions on page 168. ◆

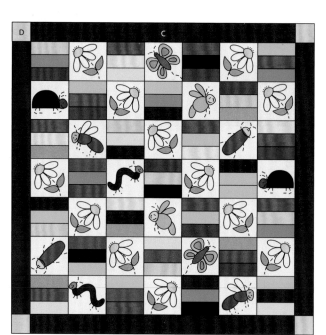

**Cute as a Bug Baby Quilt**
Placement Diagram 48" x 48"

**Outline Stitch**

**Running Stitch**

**Stem Stitch**

**French Knot**

**Wings**
Cut 2 each white tonal
(reverse 1 of each)

③

②

**Head**
Cut 2 green tonal
(reverse 1)

Center

**Body**
Cut 2 red/green print
(reverse 1)

④

⑤

①

**Tail**
Cut 2 red tonal
(reverse 1)

**Bug 3**
Make 2
(reverse 1)

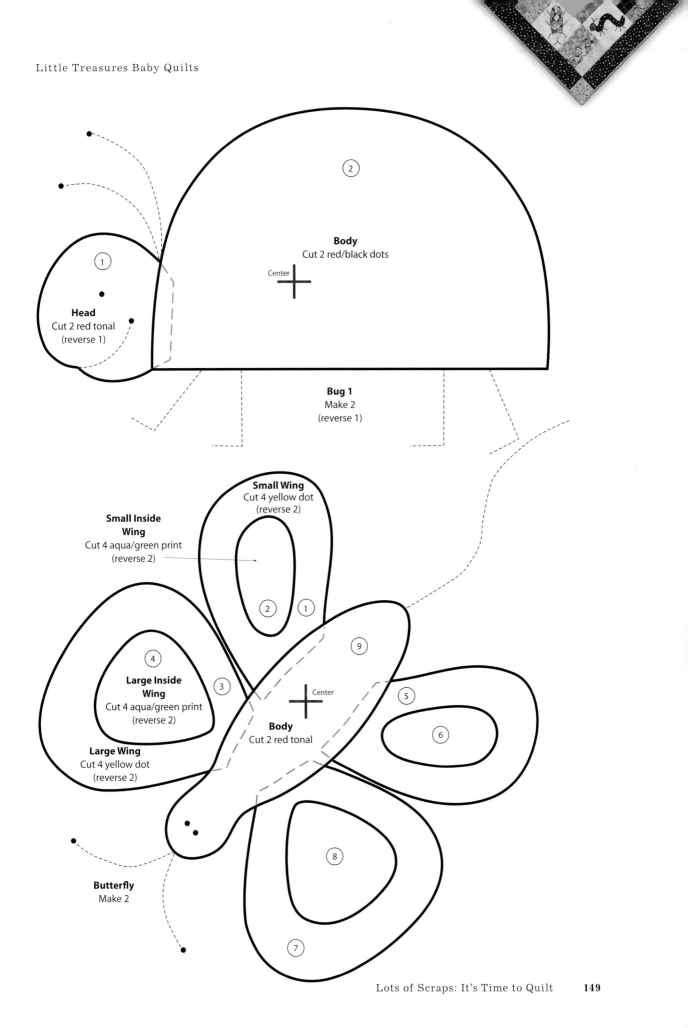

**Body**
Cut 2 red/black dots

Center

**Head**
Cut 2 red tonal
(reverse 1)

**Bug 1**
Make 2
(reverse 1)

**Small Wing**
Cut 4 yellow dot
(reverse 2)

**Small Inside Wing**
Cut 4 aqua/green print
(reverse 2)

**Large Inside Wing**
Cut 4 aqua/green print
(reverse 2)

**Large Wing**
Cut 4 yellow dot
(reverse 2)

**Body**
Cut 2 red tonal

Center

**Butterfly**
Make 2

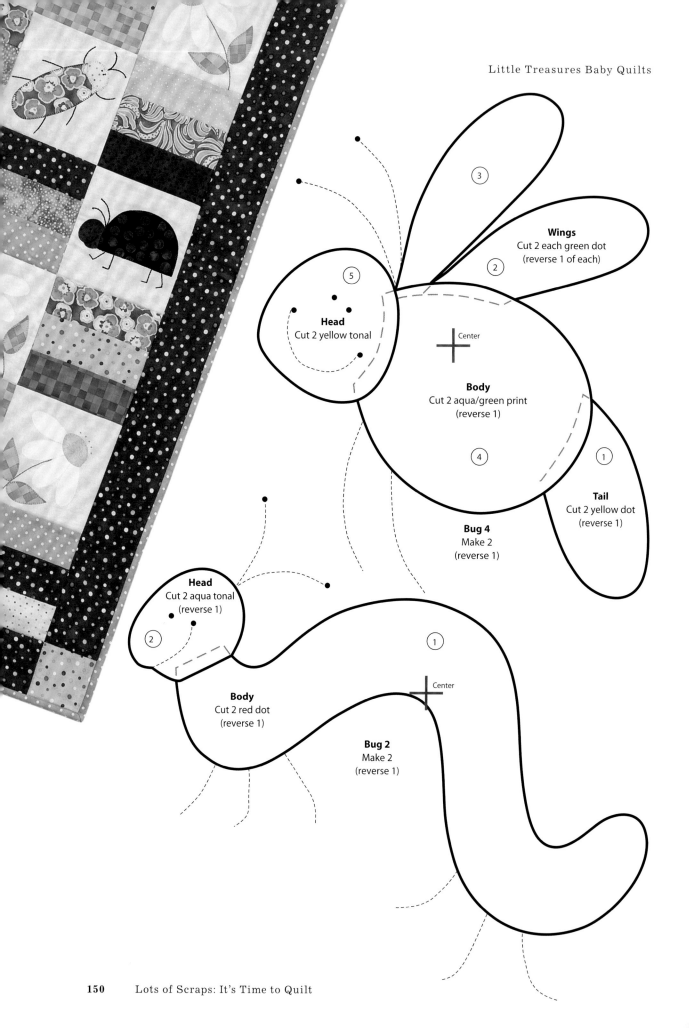

3

**Wings**
Cut 2 each green dot
(reverse 1 of each)

2

5

**Head**
Cut 2 yellow tonal

Center

**Body**
Cut 2 aqua/green print
(reverse 1)

4

1

**Tail**
Cut 2 yellow dot
(reverse 1)

**Bug 4**
Make 2
(reverse 1)

**Head**
Cut 2 aqua tonal
(reverse 1)

2

1

Center

**Body**
Cut 2 red dot
(reverse 1)

**Bug 2**
Make 2
(reverse 1)

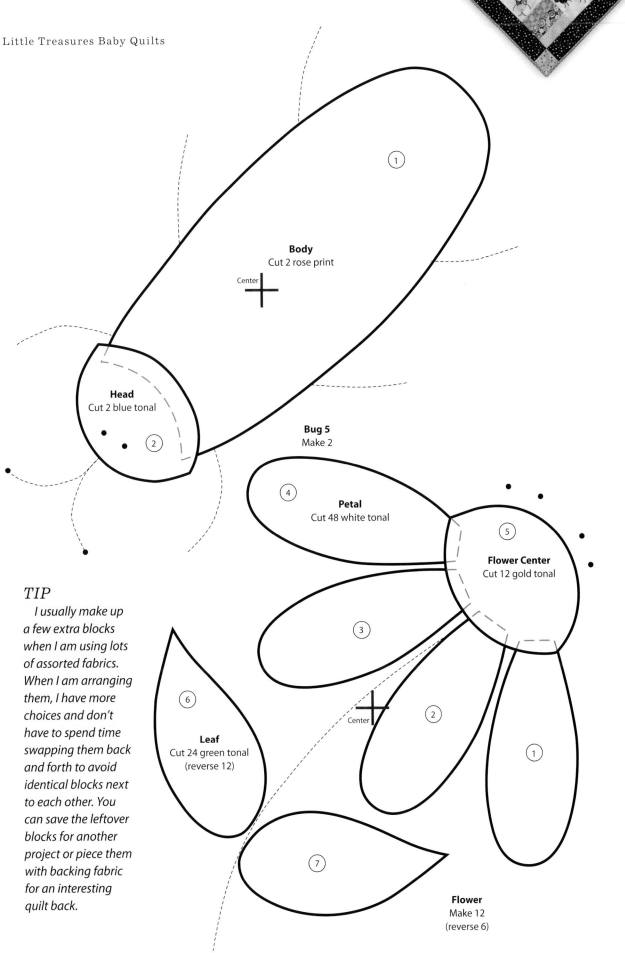

**Body**
Cut 2 rose print

Center

**Head**
Cut 2 blue tonal

2

**Bug 5**
Make 2

4

**Petal**
Cut 48 white tonal

5

**Flower Center**
Cut 12 gold tonal

3

*TIP*

*I usually make up a few extra blocks when I am using lots of assorted fabrics. When I am arranging them, I have more choices and don't have to spend time swapping them back and forth to avoid identical blocks next to each other. You can save the leftover blocks for another project or piece them with backing fabric for an interesting quilt back.*

6

**Leaf**
Cut 24 green tonal
(reverse 12)

Center

2

1

7

**Flower**
Make 12
(reverse 6)

# Hearts A-Flutter Baby Quilt

Design by RUTH SWASEY

This cute little quilt uses reproduction children's prints copied from those popular in the 1930s.

## Project Specifications

Skill Level: Beginner
Quilt Size: 49" x 59"
Block Size: 5" x 5"
Number of Blocks: 36

**Heart**
5" x 5" Block
Make 36

| FABRIC Measurements based on 42" usable fabric width. | #STRIPS & PIECES | CUT | #PIECES | SUBCUT |
|---|---|---|---|---|
| Assorted scraps 1930s reproduction prints | 48 | 5" squares for heart appliqué | | |
| | 69 | 2½" x 5½" B rectangles | | |
| | 86 | 2½" C squares | | |
| | | 2¼" strips to total 260" for binding | | |
| 1⅞ yards white print | 6 | 5½" x 42" | 36 | 5½" A squares |
| | 5 | 5½" x 42" D | | |
| Backing | | 55" x 65" | | |

## SUPPLIES

- Batting 55" x 65"
- Cream all-purpose thread
- Quilting thread
- 1¾ yards 12"-wide fusible web
- 1⅞ yards fabric stabilizer
- Basic sewing tools and supplies

## Completing the Blocks

**Step 1.** Trace 48 heart shapes, from template on page 173, onto the paper side of the fusible web; cut out each shape, leaving a margin around each one.

**Step 2.** Cut away the fusible web from the center of each heart shape leaving a ⅜" area all around as shown in Figure 1. *Note: Cutting away the fusible web from the heart centers reduces the bulk and stiffness sometimes created by using fusible web.*

**Figure 1**

**Step 3.** Fuse the heart-outline shapes onto the wrong side of the 5" scrap squares; cut out shapes around outside marked lines.

**Step 4.** Remove paper backing from each cut shape.

**Step 5.** Fold each A square in quarters and crease lightly to mark center. Center and fuse one heart shape to each A square; set aside the remaining 12 heart shapes for quilt borders.

**Step 6.** Cut (48) 5" squares fabric stabilizer; set aside 12 squares for borders.

**Step 7.** Pin a stabilizer square to the wrong side of each fused A square.

**Step 8.** Using cream thread and a machine buttonhole stitch, machine-stitch around each heart shape to secure in place.

**Step 9.** Remove fabric stabilizer after stitching is complete to finish the 36 Heart blocks.

## Completing the Quilt

**Step 1.** Join nine Heart blocks to make a vertical row referring to the Placement Diagram for positioning; press seams in one direction. Repeat to make four vertical block rows.

**Step 2.** Join 23 B rectangles on the 5½" sides to make a B strip; press seams in one direction. Trim the strip to 45½". Repeat to make three B strips. **Note:** *You may trim an equal amount off both ends of each strip or all on one end as in the sample quilt.*

**Step 3.** Join 23 C squares to make a C strip; trim the strip to 45½". Repeat to make two C strips.

**Step 4.** Join the C strips with the block strips and the B strips referring to Figure 2; press seams toward the B and C strips.

**Step 5.** Join 20 C squares to make the top strip; press seams in one direction. Trim strip to 39½"; repeat to make the bottom strip.

**Step 6.** Sew the C strips to the top and the bottom of the pieced center; press seams toward C strips.

**Step 7.** Join the D strips with right sides together on short ends to make one long strip; press seams open. Subcut strip into four 49½" D strips.

**Step 8.** Sew a D strip to opposite long sides and one to the top and bottom of the pieced center; press seams toward D strips.

**Step 9.** Arrange and fuse one heart shape in each corner and one at each end of each D strip as shown in Figure 3; pin a stabilizer square behind each shape and machine-stitch in place as for blocks to complete the pieced top. Remove stabilizer.

**Figure 3**

**Step 10.** Finish the quilt referring to the Finishing Instructions on page 168. ◆

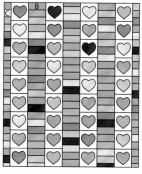

**Figure 2**

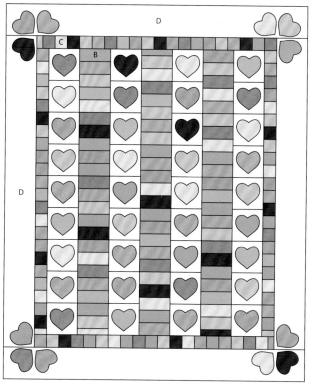

**Hearts-A-Flutter Baby Quilt**
Placement Diagram 49" x 59"

# Look at Me!

Design by CONNIE KAUFFMAN

## Make an eye spy-like quilt a toddler will love.

## Project Specifications
Skill Level: Beginner
Quilt Size: 38" x 48"

## Completing the Appliqué
**Step 1.** Trace the appliqué shapes onto the paper side of the fusible web as directed on pattern; cut out shapes leaving a margin around each one.

**Step 2.** Fuse shapes to the wrong side of the assorted novelty print scraps; cut out shapes on traced lines.

**Step 3.** Remove paper backing from the large appliqué shapes.

**Step 4.** Center and fuse a large appliqué shape to each A square referring to the quilt photo for positioning.

**Step 5.** Remove paper backing from the heart shapes; center and fuse a heart on each fused shape referring to the quilt photo for positioning suggestions.

**Step 6.** Cut (17) 5" x 5" squares fabric stabilizer; pin a square to the wrong side of each fused A square.

**Step 7.** Using thread to match fabrics, machine buttonhole-stitch around each fused appliqué shape.

**Step 8.** Remove pins and fabric stabilizer to complete the appliquéd A squares.

| FABRIC Measurements based on 42" usable fabric width. | #STRIPS & PIECES | CUT |
|---|---|---|
| Assorted novelty print scraps | 17 | 5½" B squares |
| | 20 | 4½" x 5½" G rectangles |
| | 4 | 4½" x 7" H rectangles |
| | 4 | 4½" x 8" I rectangles |
| | | Appliqué pieces as per patterns |
| Assorted white tonals | 17 | 5½" A squares |
| ⅓ yard orange mottled | 2 | 1½" x 27½" D |
| | 2 | 1½" x 35½" C |
| ⅜ yard lime green tonal | 2 | 2" x 37½" E |
| | 2 | 2" x 30½" F |
| ½ yard coordinating bright print | 5 | 2¼" x 42" binding |
| Backing | | 44" x 54" |

### SUPPLIES
- Batting 44" x 54"
- All-purpose thread to match fabrics
- Quilting thread
- ¾ yard fusible web
- ¾ yard fabric stabilizer
- Basic sewing tools and supplies

## Completing the Quilt
**Step 1.** Join two appliquéd A squares with three B squares to make a row; press seams toward B. Repeat to make four rows.

**Step 2.** Join three appliquéd A squares with two B squares to make a row; press seams toward B. Repeat to make three rows.

**Step 3.** Referring to the Placement Diagram for positioning, join the rows to complete the pieced center; press seams in one direction.

**Step 4.** Sew C strips to opposite long sides and D strips to the top and bottom of the pieced center; press seams toward C and D strips.

**Step 5.** Repeat Step 4 with E and then F strips, pressing seams toward E and F after stitching.

**Step 6.** Join five G rectangles with two I rectangles to make a side strip; press seams in one direction. Repeat to make two side strips.

**Step 7.** Sew a side strip to opposite long sides of the

pieced center; press seams toward side strips.

**Step 8.** Join five G rectangles with two H rectangles to make the top strip; press seams in one direction. Repeat to make the bottom strip.

**Step 9.** Sew the top strip to the top and the bottom strip to the bottom of the pieced center to complete the top; press seams in one direction.

**Step 10.** Finish the quilt referring to the Finishing Instructions on page 168. ◆

**Look at Me!**
Placement Diagram 38" x 48"

**Appliqué Shape**
Cut 17 assorted novelty print scraps

**Heart**
Cut 17 assorted
novelty print scraps

# Choo-Choo Baby Quilt

Design by BARBARA CLAYTON

Any little boy will love to be tucked in under this train-design quilt.

## Project Specifications

Skill Level: Advanced
Quilt Size: 41" x 41" without
   prairie points
Block Size: 9" x 9"
Number of Blocks: 9

**Choo-Choo**
9" x 9" Block
Make 4

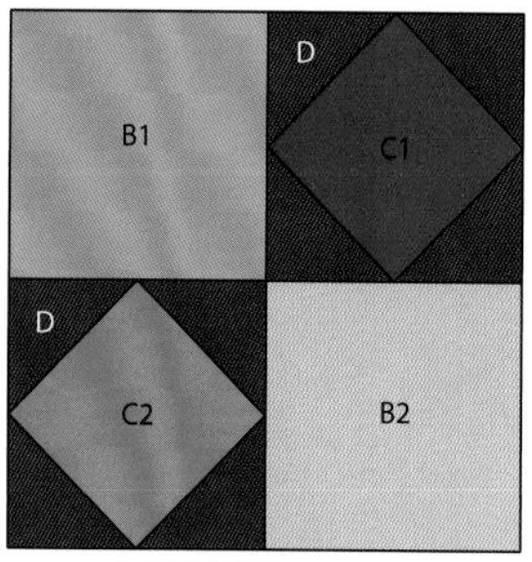

**Diagonal Squares**
9" x 9" Block
Make 1

| FABRIC<br>Measurements based on 42" usable fabric width. | #STRIPS & PIECES | CUT | #PIECES | SUBCUT |
|---|---|---|---|---|
| Red, blue and orange scraps | 3<br>3 | 5" red C1 squares<br>5" orange C2 squares<br>Appliqué pieces as per patterns | | |
| ¼ yard light green print | 1 | 5" x 42" | 4 | 5" B2 squares |
| ¼ yard yellow print | 1 | 5¾" x 42"<br><br><br>Appliqué pieces as per patterns | 2 | 5¾" squares; cut on both diagonals to make 8 F triangles |
| ¼ yard red dot | 1 | 3½" x 42" | 8<br>4 | 3½" M squares<br>2½" J squares |
| ⅜ yard light blue print | 1 | 9½" x 42" | 4 | 9½" A squares |
| ½ yard green mottled | 4 | 2½" x 42"<br><br>Appliqué pieces as per patterns | 4<br>4 | 31½" I strips<br>2½" H squares |
| ⅝ yard navy plaid | 2 | 7" x 42"<br>Appliqué pieces as per pattern | 16 | 3½" K rectangles |
| ¾ yard black solid | 3<br>1 | 2¾" x 42"<br>5¾" x 42"<br><br><br><br><br>Appliqué pieces as per patterns | 24<br>2 | 2¾" D squares<br>5¾" squares; cut in half on both diagonals to make 8 E triangles |
| 1⅛ yards medium blue tonal | 1<br>8 | 5" x 42"<br>3½" x 42" | 6<br>8<br>84 | 5" B1 squares<br>3½" L squares<br>3½" N squares |
| Backing | | 42" x 42" | | |

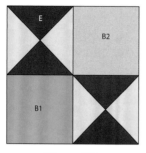

**Diagonal X's**
9" x 9" Block
Make 2

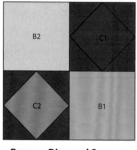

**Reverse Diagonal Squares**
9" x 9" Block
Make 1

**Center**
9" x 9" Block
Make 1

## Completing the Choo-Choo Blocks

**Step 1.** Trace the train appliqué shapes onto the paper side of the freezer paper as directed on pattern for number to cut. **Note:** *To reduce cutting, you may trace the shapes onto one piece of freezer paper and layer with multiple pieces to cut more than one piece at a time. Be sure to pin the layers together to hold for accurate cutting.*
**Step 2.** Press the waxy side of the freezer-paper shapes to the

### SUPPLIES

- Batting 42" x 42"
- All-purpose thread to match fabrics
- Quilting thread
- Water-soluble marker
- Water-soluble glue stick
- Freezer paper
- Sponge or cloth
- Basic sewing tools and supplies

wrong side of fabrics as directed on pattern for color.
**Step 3.** Cut out each shape leaving ¼" all around for turn-under seam allowance; clip into curves, points and indentations almost to the paper patterns.
**Step 4.** Using a glue stick, glue the seam allowance over the edge and to the back of the freezer paper; glue all the way around each piece except for edges marked by dashed gray lines on the pattern.
**Step 5.** Trace the quilting design lines onto the train engines, smoke stacks, windows, wheels, headlights and cowcatchers with the water-soluble marker.
**Step 6.** Using the full-size pattern as a guide, pin the appliqué pieces together in numerical order, overlapping pieces as necessary; stitch together along the overlapping edges of each piece with a narrow blind-hem stitch and clear nylon thread.
**Step 7.** Fold each A square and crease to mark the vertical and horizontal centers.
**Step 8.** Center a train motif on each A square and stitch in place as in Step 6 to complete the blocks.
**Step 9.** Turn each block wrong side up and make a slit behind the train motif; trim away the backing to ¼" from the edge of the stitching around the train motif.

**Step 10.** Use a sponge or cloth to wet the back of each train appliqué. Tear away the freezer paper from behind each motif; let dry and press lightly.

## Completing the Diagonal Squares & Center Blocks

**Step 1.** Mark a diagonal line from corner to corner on the wrong side of each D square.
**Step 2.** Place a D square on opposite corners of C1 and stitch on the marked lines as shown in Figure 1; trim seams to ¼" and press D to the right side, again referring to Figure 1.

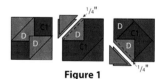

**Figure 1**

**Step 3.** Repeat Step 2 on the remaining corners of C to complete a C1-D unit as shown in Figure 2; repeat to complete three each C1-D and C2-D units, again referring to Figure 2.

**Figure 2**

**Step 4.** To complete the Diagonal Squares block, sew one C1-D unit to B1 as shown in Figure 3 to complete a B-C-D1 row; press seam toward B.

Repeat to make a B-C-D2 row, again referring to Figure 3.

**Figure 3**

**Step 5.** Join the B-C-D rows referring to the block drawing to complete one block.

**Step 6.** Repeat Steps 4 and 5 to complete the Reverse Diagonal Squares block referring to the block drawing for positioning of pieces.

**Step 7.** Repeat Steps 4 and 5 with two B1 squares to complete the Center block referring to the block drawing for positioning of pieces.

## Completing the Diagonal X's Blocks

**Step 1.** Sew E to F as shown in Figure 4; press seams toward E. Repeat to make eight E-F units.

**Figure 4**

**Step 2.** Join two E-F units to make a square unit as shown in Figure 5; press seam in one direction. Repeat to make four square units.

**Figure 5**

**Step 3.** To complete one Diagonal X's block, sew a square unit to B1 to make a row as shown in Figure 6; press seam toward B1. Repeat with B2 to make a row, again

referring to Figure 6; press seam toward B2.

**Figure 6**

**Step 4.** Join the rows to complete one block referring to the block drawing; press seam in one direction.

**Step 5.** Repeat Steps 3 and 4 to complete two blocks.

## Completing the Quilt

**Step 1.** Join one each Diagonal X's, Choo-Choo and Diagonal Squares blocks with two G strips to make the X row referring to Figure 7; press seams toward G strips.

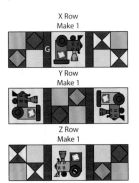

X Row
Make 1

Y Row
Make 1

Z Row
Make 1

**Figure 7**

**Step 2.** Join two Choo-Choo blocks with the Center block and two G strips to make the Y row, again referring to Figure 7; press seams toward G strips.

**Step 3.** Join one each Diagonal X's, Choo-Choo and Reverse Diagonal Squares blocks to make the Z row, again referring

to Figure 7; press seams toward G strips.

**Step 4.** Join three G strips with two H squares to make a sashing row as shown in Figure 8; press seams toward G strips.

G    H

**Figure 8**

**Step 5.** Join the X, Y and Z rows with the sashing rows referring to the Placement Diagram to complete the pieced center; press seams toward sashing rows.

**Step 6.** Sew an I strip to opposite sides of the pieced center; press seams toward I strips.

**Step 7.** Sew a J square to each end of each remaining I strip; press seams away from J. Sew the I-J strips to the remaining sides of the pieced center; press seams toward I-J strips.

**Step 8.** Join four K rectangles with one L and two M squares as shown in Figure 9; press seams toward K. Repeat to make four K-L-M strips. Sew an L square to each end of two of the strips; press seams away from L.

**Figure 9**

**Step 9.** Sew the shorter K-L-M strips to opposite sides and the longer strips to the remaining sides of the pieced center; press seams toward the K-L-M strips.

**Step 10.** Fold each N square in half on one diagonal and in half again as shown in Figure 10; press to make prairie points.

**Figure 10**

**Step 11.** Evenly arrange and pin 21 prairie points along each side of the pieced center, overlapping them about 1½" as shown in Figure 11; machine-baste in place when satisfied with placement.

1½"

**Figure 11**

**Step 12.** Place the quilt top and batting right sides together with prairie points tucked inside; pin batting to the pinned layers. Smooth and stitch all around, leaving 8" open on one side for turning.

**Step 13.** Trim batting close to seam; turn right side out through the opening. Turn opening to the inside and hand-stitch closed.

**Step 14.** Press edges flat; pin or baste layers together for quilting.

**Step 15.** Using clear nylon thread, machine-quilt in the ditch of all seams. Hand-quilt on marked detail lines and as desired to finish. ◆

**Choo-Choo Baby Quilt**
Placement Diagram 41" x 41" without prairie points

*TIP*

*Save ends of binding strips leftover from every quilt and join together as you save to make a continuous strip. This will come in handy when you are ready to bind your next scrap quilt.*

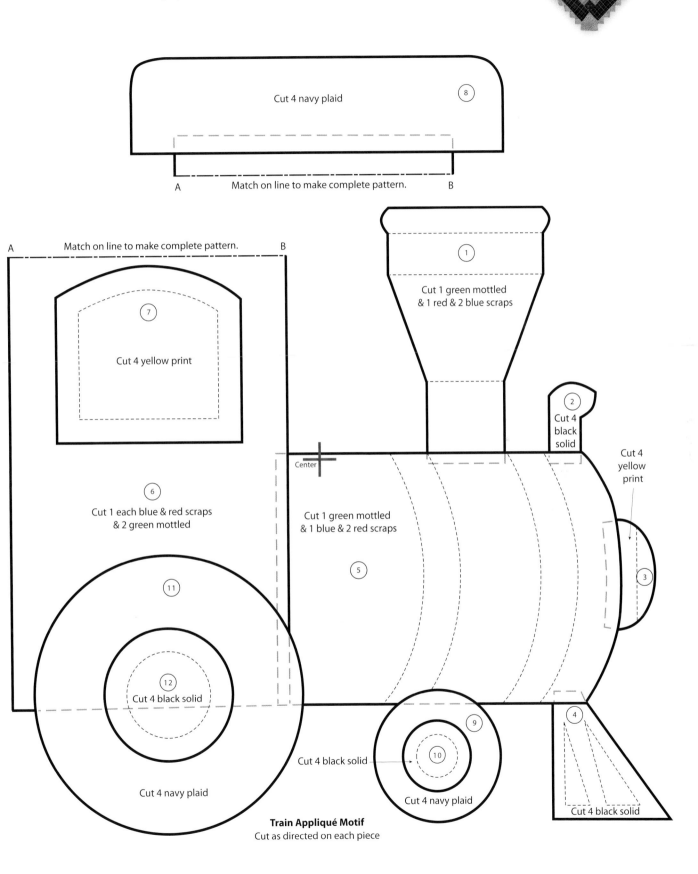

Cut 4 navy plaid

⑧

A          Match on line to make complete pattern.          B

A          Match on line to make complete pattern.          B

⑦

Cut 4 yellow print

①

Cut 1 green mottled
& 1 red & 2 blue scraps

②

Cut 4
black
solid

Cut 4
yellow
print

⑥

Cut 1 each blue & red scraps
& 2 green mottled

Center

Cut 1 green mottled
& 1 blue & 2 red scraps

⑤

③

⑪

⑫

Cut 4 black solid

⑨

⑩

Cut 4 black solid

④

Cut 4 navy plaid

Cut 4 navy plaid

Cut 4 black solid

**Train Appliqué Motif**
Cut as directed on each piece

# Fish & Bubbles

Design by CAROLYN S. VAGTS

Add circles in a variety of sizes to create the bubbles shown on the plain squares in this playful quilt.

## Project Specifications

Skill Level: Beginner
Quilt Size: 43½" x 55½"
Block Size: 12" x 12" and 6" x 6"
Number of Blocks: 3 and 18

**Fish**
12" x 12" Block
Make 3
Reverse 1

**Four-Patch**
6" x 6" Block
Make 18

| FABRIC<br>Measurements based on 42" usable fabric width. | #STRIPS & PIECES | CUT | #PIECES | SUBCUT |
|---|---|---|---|---|
| ■ Scrap black solid | | Appliqué pieces as per pattern | | |
| Assorted pale blue, blue and blue/green batik scraps | | Appliqué circles as desired | | |
| Assorted blue and green batik scraps | 72 | 3½" C squares | | |
| Lavender, yellow, green and blue batik scraps | | Appliqué pieces as per pattern | | |
| ¼ yard royal blue batik | 2<br>3 | 1¼" x 36½" D<br>1¼" x 42" E | | |
| ¾ yard blue batik | 2<br>3<br>5 | 3½" x 38" F<br>3½" x 42" G<br>2¼" x 42" binding | | |
| 1⅛ yards sea green batik | 1<br>3 | 12½" x 42"<br>6½" x 42" | 3<br>18 | 12½" A squares<br>6½" B squares |
| Backing | | 50" x 62" | | |

### SUPPLIES

- Batting 50" x 62"
- All-purpose thread to match fabrics
- Quilting thread
- 1½ yards fusible web
- Basic sewing tools and supplies

## Project Note

Batik fabrics do not fray as much as some other cottons so they work very well for machine-appliqué motifs.

## Completing the Appliquéd Blocks

**Step 1.** Trace fish and circle shapes onto the paper side of the fusible web; cut out shapes, leaving a margin around each one.

**Step 2.** Fuse shapes to the wrong side of fabrics as directed on each piece for color and number to cut; cut out shapes on traced lines. Remove paper backing.

**Step 3.** Fold each A square in half and crease to mark the vertical and horizontal centers.

**Step 4.** Center, arrange and fuse the fish shapes on A in numerical order referring to the pattern.

**Step 5.** Arrange and fuse the circle shapes on the B squares

referring to the Placement Diagram for positioning.

**Step 6.** Straight stitch around edges of each fused shape with thread to match fabrics to complete the Fish blocks and B squares.

## Completing the Four-Patch Blocks

**Step 1.** To complete one Four-Patch block, join two C squares to make a row; press seam in one direction. Repeat to make two rows.

**Step 2.** Join the rows with seams in alternating directions to complete one Four-Patch block; repeat to make 18 blocks.

## Completing the Quilt

**Step 1.** Referring to Figure 1, arrange and join the Fish and Four-Patch blocks with B squares in rows and sections; press seams toward B and Fish blocks.

**Step 2.** Join the rows and sections, again referring to Figure 1, to complete the pieced center; press seams in one direction.

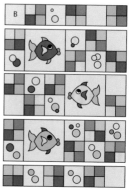

**Figure 1**

**Step 3.** Sew a D strip to the top and bottom of the pieced center; press seams toward D strips.

**Step 4.** Join the E strips on short ends to make one long strip; press seams open. Subcut strip into two 50" E strips.

**Step 5.** Sew the E strips to opposite long sides of the pieced center; press seams toward E strips.

**Step 6.** Sew an F strip to the top and bottom of the pieced center; press seams toward F strips.

**Step 7.** Join the G strips on short ends to make one long strip; press seams open. Subcut strip into two 56" G strips.

**Step 8.** Sew a G strip to the top and bottom of the pieced center to complete the pieced top; press seams toward G strips.

**Step 9.** Finish the quilt referring to the Finishing Instructions on page 168. ◆

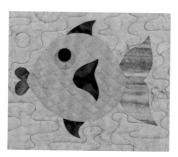

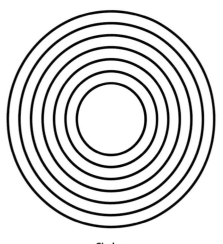

**Circles**
Cut assorted pale blue, blue & blue/green scraps in a variety of sizes

**Fish & Bubbles**
Placement Diagram 43½" x 55½"

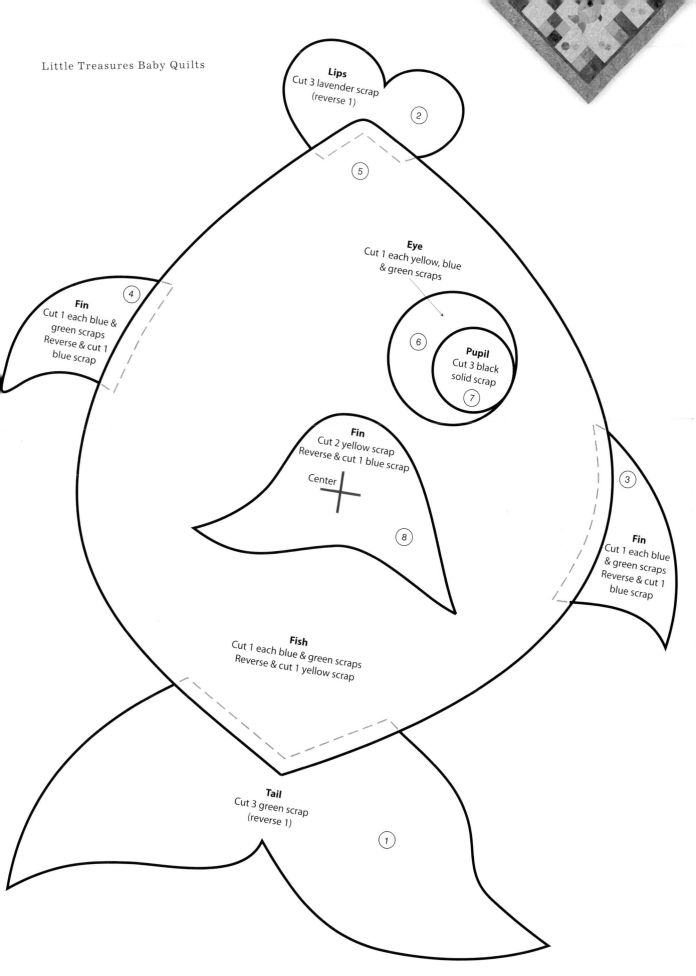

**Lips**
Cut 3 lavender scrap
(reverse 1)

②

⑤

**Eye**
Cut 1 each yellow, blue
& green scraps

**Fin**
Cut 1 each blue &
green scraps
Reverse & cut 1
blue scrap

④

⑥

**Pupil**
Cut 3 black
solid scrap

⑦

**Fin**
Cut 2 yellow scrap
Reverse & cut 1 blue scrap

Center

⑧

③

**Fin**
Cut 1 each blue
& green scraps
Reverse & cut 1
blue scrap

**Fish**
Cut 1 each blue & green scraps
Reverse & cut 1 yellow scrap

**Tail**
Cut 3 green scrap
(reverse 1)

①

# Finishing Instructions

## Completing Your Quilt
### Choosing a Quilting Design

There are several types of quilting designs, some of which may not have to be marked. The easiest of the unmarked designs is in-the-ditch quilting. Here the quilting stitches are placed in the valley created by the seams joining two pieces together, or next to the edge of an appliqué design. Machine quilters choose this option because the stitches are not as obvious on the finished quilt (Figure 1).

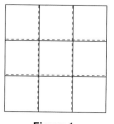

**Figure 1**

Outline-quilting ¼" or more away from seams or appliqué shapes is another no-mark alternative (Figure 2) that prevents having to sew through the layers made by seams, thus making stitching easier.

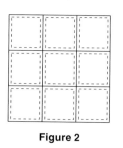

**Figure 2**

Meander or free-motion quilting by machine (Figure 3)

fills in open spaces and doesn't require marking. It is fun and easy to stitch.

**Figure 3**

### Marking the Top for Quilting

If you choose a fancy or allover design for quilting, you will need to transfer the design to your quilt top before layering with the backing and batting.

Use a sharp medium-lead or silver pencil on light background fabrics. Test the pencil marks to guarantee that they will wash out of your quilt top when quilting is complete, or be sure your quilting stitches cover the pencil marks. Mechanical pencils with very fine points may be used successfully to mark quilts.

Manufactured quilting-design templates are available in many designs and sizes, and are cut out of a durable plastic template material that is easy to use.

No matter what marking method you use, remember— the marked lines should never show on the finished quilt. When the top is marked, it is ready for layering.

### Preparing the Quilt Backing

A backing is generally cut at least 6" larger than the quilt top or 3" larger on all sides. For a 64" x 78" finished quilt, the backing would need to be at least 70" x 84".

To avoid having the seam down the center of the back, cut two fabric pieces the length of the backing needed; cut or tear one of these pieces in half, and sew half to each side of the second piece as shown in Figure 4.

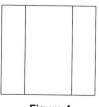

**Figure 4**

Quilt backings that are more than 88" wide may be pieced in horizontal pieces as shown in Figure 5.

**Figure 5**

### Layering the Quilt Sandwich

Layering the quilt top with the batting and backing is time-consuming. Open the batting several days before you need it and place over a bed or flat on the floor to help flatten the creases caused from folds.

Iron the backing piece, folding in half both vertically and horizontally, and pressing to mark the centers.

**If you are quilting in a frame,** place the backing in the frame, right side down. Place the batting on the backing, smoothing out wrinkles. Trim batting to match backing. Pin quilt top right side up on batting, adjusting to be sure blocks are square.

**If you are quilting in a hoop,** place the ironed backing right side down on a clean floor or table. Place the batting on top of the backing, smoothing out any wrinkles. Trim the batting to the same size as the backing. Place the quilt top on top of the batting, wrong side against the batting. Working from the center to the outside edges, smooth out any wrinkles or lumps.

To hold the quilt layers together for quilting, baste by hand or use safety pins. If basting by hand, thread a long thin needle with a long piece of unknotted white or off-white thread. Starting in the center and leaving a long tail, make 4"–6"-long stitches toward the outside edge of the quilt top, smoothing as you baste. Start at the center again and work toward the outside as shown in Figure 6.

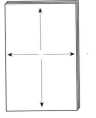

**Figure 6**

If quilting by machine, you may prefer to use safety pins to hold your fabric sandwich together. Follow instructions for quilting in a hoop, substituting pins for needle and thread. To use pins, start in the center of the quilt and pin to the outside, leaving pins open until all are placed. When you are satisfied that all layers are smooth, close the pins. To use basting spray, follow the manufacturer's instructions on the container.

## Quilting
### Hand Quilting

Hand quilting is the process of placing stitches through the quilt top, batting and backing to hold them together. While it serves a functional purpose, it also adds beauty and loft to the finished quilt.

To begin, thread a sharp between needle with an 18" piece of quilting thread. Tie a small knot in the end of the thread. Position the needle about ½"–1" away from the starting point on the quilt top. Sink needle through the top into the batting layer but not through the backing. Pull the needle up at the starting point of the quilting design. Pull the needle and thread until the knot sinks through the top into the batting (Figure 7).

**Figure 7**

Take small, even running stitches along the marked quilting line (Figure 8). Keep one hand positioned underneath to feel the needle go all the way through to the backing.

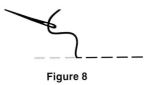

**Figure 8**

When you have nearly run out of thread, wind the thread around the needle several times to make a small knot and pull it close to the fabric. Insert the needle into the fabric on the quilting line and come out with the needle ½"–1" away, pulling the knot into the fabric layers the same as when you started. Pull and cut thread close to fabric. The end should disappear inside after cutting.

### Machine Quilting

Successful machine quilting requires practice. Special machine-quilting needles work best to penetrate the three layers in your quilt.

Prepare the quilt for machine quilting in the same way as for hand quilting. Use safety pins to hold the layers together instead of basting with thread.

Presser-foot quilting is best used for straight-line quilting because the presser bar lever does not need to be continually lifted. Set the machine on a longer stitch length (3.0 or 8–10 stitches to the inch). Too tight a stitch causes puckering and fabric tucks, either on the quilt top or backing. An even-feed or walking foot helps to eliminate the tucks and puckering by feeding the upper and lower layers through the machine evenly. Before you begin, loosen the amount of pressure on the presser foot.

For free-motion quilting, use your machine's darning foot with the feed dogs down. Refer to your sewing machine manual for other special instructions. Practice on a sample before trying this method on your quilt.

**Finishing the Edges**
After your quilt is quilted, the edges need to be finished, but you must decide how you want the edges of your quilt finished before layering the backing and batting with the quilt top.

**Without Binding— Self-Finish**
There are several ways to eliminate adding an edge finish. This is done before quilting.

**Method 1: Create a pocket**
**1.** Place the batting on a flat surface.
**2.** Place the pieced top right side up on the batting.
**3.** Place the backing right sides together with the pieced top.
**4.** Pin and/or baste the layers together to hold flat referring to Layering the Quilt Sandwich.
**5.** Begin stitching in the center of one side using a ¼" seam allowance, reversing at the beginning and end of the seam. Continue stitching all around and back to the beginning side. Leave a 12" or larger opening. Clip corners to reduce excess.
**6.** Turn right side out through the opening.

**7.** Turn the raw edges in ¼" and slipstitch the opening closed by hand. The quilt may now be quilted by hand or machine.

The disadvantage to this method is that once the edges are stitched, any creases or wrinkles that might form during the quilting process cannot be flattened out. Tying is the preferred method for finishing a quilt constructed using this method.

**Method 2: Use the backing**
Bringing the backing fabric to the front is another method of self-finishing.
**1.** Complete the quilt as for hand or machine quilting.
**2.** Trim only the batting even with the quilt top. Trim the backing 1" larger than the completed top all around.
**3.** Turn the backing edge ½" to the wrong side; fold to overlap onto the front of the quilt ¼".
**4.** Machine-stitch close to the edge through all layers, or blind-stitch in place to finish.

**Method 3: Use the top**
The front may be turned to the back. If using this method, a wider front border is needed.
**1.** Trim the backing and batting 1" smaller than the top.
**2.** Turn the top edge under ½" and then turn to the back.
**3.** Stitch in place.

**Method 4: Stitch top and back together**
The top and backing may be stitched together by hand at the edge. To accomplish this,

quilting must be stopped ½" from the quilt-top edge.
**1.** Trim the top and backing even and trim the batting to ¼"–½" smaller.
**2.** Turn under the edges of the top and backing ¼"–½"
**3.** Blind-stitch top and backing together at the very edge.

These methods do not require the use of extra fabric and save time in preparation of binding strips; they are not as durable as an added binding.

**Binding**
The technique of adding extra fabric at the edges of the quilt is called binding. The binding encloses the edges and adds an extra layer of fabric for durability. The instructions given with most of the projects in this book list cutting for a number of 2¼"-wide binding strips. Use these strips and follow the instructions for double-fold, straight-grain binding.

To prepare a quilt for the addition of the binding, trim the batting and backing layers even with the top of the quilt using a rotary cutter and ruler, or shears. Using a walking-foot attachment (sometimes called an even-feed foot attachment), machine-baste the three layers together all around approximately ⅛" from the cut edge.

Bias binding may be purchased in packages in many different colors but is not always available in a color to match your quilt. The advantage to self-made binding is that you can use fabrics from your quilt to coordinate colors.

Double-fold, straight-grain binding and double-fold, bias-grain binding are two of the most commonly used types of binding.

Double-fold, straight-grain binding is commonly used on the edges of quilts with square corners. Double-fold, bias-grain binding is best suited for quilts with rounded corners or scalloped edges.

## Straight-Grain Binding

To make double-fold, straight-grain binding, cut 2¼"-wide strips of fabric across the width or down the length of the fabric totaling the perimeter of the quilt plus 12". The strips are joined as shown in Figure 9 and pressed in half wrong sides together along the length using an iron on a cotton setting with no steam.

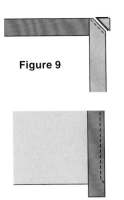

**Figure 9**

**Figure 10**

## Applying Binding Using Mitered Corners

**1.** Lining up the raw edges, place the binding on the top of the quilt and begin sewing (again using the walking foot) approximately 6" from the beginning of the binding strip. Stop sewing ¼" from the first corner, leave the needle in the quilt, turn and sew diagonally to the corner as shown in Figure 10.
**2.** Fold the binding at a 45-degree angle up and away from the quilt as shown in Figure 11 and back down even with the raw edge of the next side of the quilt.

**Figure 11**

**3.** Starting at the top raw edge of the quilt, begin sewing the next side as shown in Figure 12. Repeat at the next three corners.

**Figure 12**

**4.** As you approach the beginning of the binding strip, stop stitching and overlap the binding ends ½"; trim. Join the two ends with a ¼" seam allowance and press the seam open.
**5.** Reposition the joined binding along the edge of the quilt and resume stitching to the beginning.
**6.** To finish, bring the folded edge of the binding over the raw edges and blind-stitch the binding in place over the machine-stitching line on the back side. Hand-miter the corners on the back as shown in Figure 13.

**Figure 13**

***Note:*** *Another option when you approach the beginning of the binding strip is to stop stitching and lay the end across the beginning so it will slip inside the fold. Cut the end at a 45-degree angle so the raw edges are contained inside the beginning of the strip (Figure 14). Resume stitching to the beginning. Bring the fold to the back of the quilt and hand-stitch as previously described.*

**Figure 14**

## Applying Binding Using Overlapped Corners

Overlapped corners are easier than mitered corners.
**1.** Sew binding strips to opposite sides of the quilt top.
**2.** Turn the folded edge to the back side and stitch edges down to finish.
**3.** Trim ends even.
**4.** Sew a strip to each remaining side, leaving 1½"–2" excess at each end.
**5.** Turn quilt over and fold binding end in even with previous finished edge as shown in Figure 15.

**Figure 15**

**6.** Fold binding over onto quilt back and stitch down as before, enclosing the previous bound edge in the seam as shown in Figure 16. It may be necessary to trim the folded-down section to reduce bulk.

**Figure 16**

## Bias-Grain Binding

When you are using bias-grain binding, you have the option to eliminate the corners if it doesn't interfere with the patchwork in the quilt. Round the corners off by placing a dinner plate at the corner and rotary-cutting the gentle curve (Figure 17).

**Figure 17**

## Making Bias-Grain Binding

**1.** To make double-fold, bias-grain binding, cut 2¼"-wide bias strips from the binding-fabric yardage.

**2.** Join the strips as shown in Figure 18 and press seams open.

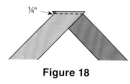

**Figure 18**

**3.** Fold the joined strips in half with wrong sides together along the length, and press with no steam as for straight-grain binding.

Follow the same procedures as previously described for sewing the binding to the quilt top.

## Making Continuous Bias Binding

Instead of cutting individual bias strips and sewing them together, you may make continuous bias binding.

**1.** Cut a square 18" x 18" from chosen binding fabric.

**2.** Cut the square in half on one diagonal to make two triangles as shown in Figure 19.

**Figure 19**

**3.** With right sides together, join the two triangles with a ¼" seam allowance as shown in Figure 20; press seam open to reduce bulk.

**Figure 20**

**4.** Mark lines every 2¼" on the wrong side of the fabric as shown in Figure 21.

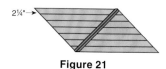

**Figure 21**

**5.** Bring the short ends right sides together, offsetting one line as shown in Figure 22; stitch to make a tube. This will seem awkward.

**Figure 22**

**6.** Begin cutting at point A as shown in Figure 23; continue cutting along marked line to make one continuous strip.

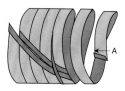

**Figure 23**

**7.** Fold strip in half along length with wrong sides together; press.

Follow the same procedures as previously described for sewing on the binding.

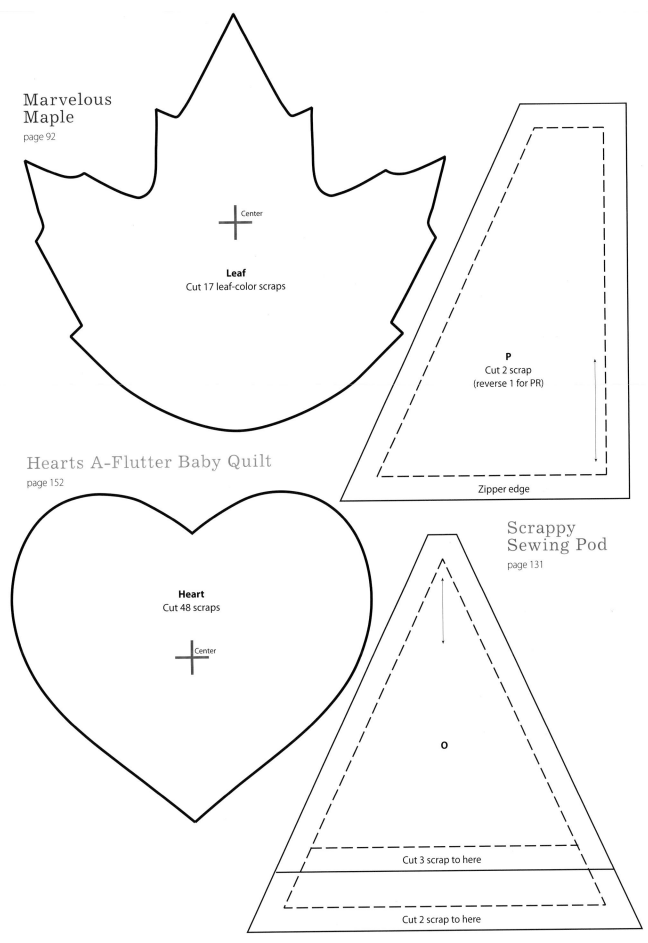

Marvelous
Maple

page 92

Center

**Leaf**
Cut 17 leaf-color scraps

**P**
Cut 2 scrap
(reverse 1 for PR)

Zipper edge

Hearts A-Flutter Baby Quilt

page 152

**Heart**
Cut 48 scraps

Center

Scrappy
Sewing Pod

page 131

**O**

Cut 3 scrap to here

Cut 2 scrap to here

# Special Thanks

We would like to thank the talented quilt designers whose work is featured in this collection.

**Pat Campbell**
Cabins From Scraps, 21

**Barbara Clayton**
A Denim Beauty, 140
Choo-Choo Baby Quilt, 158
Holly Star Wreath, 28
Starfish Beach Tote, 132

**Julia Dunn**
Halloween Spider Web, 51

**Lucy Fazely &
Michael L. Burns**
Batik Bonanza, 66
Batik Scraps, 10
March of the Crabs, 88
Twisted Spools, 18

**Sue Harvey &
Sandy Boobar**
Building Blocks, 62
Nine-Patch Weave, 55

**Sandra L. Hatch**
36-Patch Scrappy, 6
Love in a Tangle, 120
Really Scrappy Log Cabin, 33
Stars in the Crossroads, 107
Wedding Gift Bag, 136

**Connie Kauffman**
Look at Me! 155
Triangle Illusions, 116

**Chris Malone**
Cute as a Bug Baby Quilt, 145
Flowers in Bloom Tea Cozy, 124

**Connie Rand**
Dancing Colors, 14
Leftovers Squared, 24
Over & Under, 72
Tropical Fish Mats, 110

**Jill Reber**
Autumn Leaves Runner, 77
Jacob's Ladder Runner, 101

**Nancy Richoux**
Patchwork Growth Chart, 113

**Judith Sandstrom**
Marvelous Maple, 92
Scraps at the Crossroads, 69

**Christine Schultz**
Pumpkin Patch Visitors, 40

**Ruth Swasey**
Hearts A-Flutter Baby Quilt, 152
Falling Leaves, 84

**Cate Tallman-Evans**
Shiny Ornaments, 37
Under the Apple Tree, 96
Windowpanes, 58

**Carolyn S. Vagts**
Fish & Bubbles, 164

**Jodi Warner**
It's Halloween Time, 46
Scrappy Sewing Pod, 129
Colors of Autumn, 80

**Julie Weaver**
Autumn Stars Runner, 104

# Fabric & Supplies

**Page 6:** 36-Patch Scrappy—Mary Rose Fabric collection from Robert Kaufman Fabrics, Star Machine Quilting thread from Coats, Machine 60/40 Blend batting from Fairfield Processing, and OLFA rotary-cutting tools. Machine-quilted by Dianne Hodgkins.

**Page 10:** Batik Scraps—Princess Mirah Design Batik fabric from Bali Fabrics, Warm & Natural cotton batting from The Warm Co., Dual Duty Plus all-purpose thread from Coats and Quilt Basting Spray from Sullivans USA. Machine-quilted by Sharon Boensch.

**Page 14:** Dancing Colors—Cream Rose cotton batting from Mountain Mist. Machine-quilted by Carlene Corro.

**Page 18:** Twisted Spools—Classic Cotton Fabric Co. fabrics, Warm & Natural cotton batting from The Warm Co., Dual Duty Plus all-purpose and Star Machine Quilting thread from Coats and Quilt Basting Spray from Sullivans USA.

**Page 33:** Really Scrappy Log Cabin—Christmas Botanicals fabric collection from Blank Quilting, Machine 60/40 Blend batting from Fairfield Processing and Star Machine Quilting thread from Coats. Sample stitched on a Brother Innovis D sewing machine; machine-quilted by Dianne Hodgkins.

**Page 36:** Shiny Ornaments—Robert Kaufman fabrics and Poly-fil Natural cotton batting from Fairfield Processing.

**Page 55:** Nine-Patch Weave—Machine 60/40 Blend batting from Fairfield Processing and Presencia thread.

**Page 58:** Windowpanes—Fabrics from the Old Fashioned 2 Collection by Quilt Gate for Robert Kaufman Fabrics and Soft Touch batting from Fairfield Processing.

**Page 62:** Building Blocks—Tooling Around fabric collection from Blank Quilting, Machine 60/40 Blend batting from Fairfield Processing and Presencia thread.

**Page 66:** Batik Bonanza—Bali fabrics, Warm & Natural cotton batting from The Warm Co., Dual Duty Plus all-purpose and Star Machine Quilting thread from Coats and Quilt Basting Spray from Sullivans USA.

**Page 72:** Over & Under—Mountain Mist Cream Rose batting and Star Machine Quilting Thread from Coats. Professionally machine-quilted by Dianne Hodgkins.

**Page 77:** Autumn Leaves Runner—Presencia thread and Master Piece Ruler and Static Stickers.

**Page 92:** Marvelous Maple—Wonder-Under fusible web and Stitch-n-Tear fabric stabilizer from Pellon.

**Page 96:** Under the Apple Tree—Robert Kaufman fabrics and Poly-fil Natural cotton batting from Fairfield Processing.

**Page 101:** Jacob's Ladder Runner— Presencia thread and Master Piece Ruler and Static Stickers.

**Page 116:** Triangle Illusions—Hobbs Heirloom batting.

**Page 120:** Love in a Tangle—Anna Griffen's Margot Collection from Windham Fabrics, Machine 60/40 Blend batting from Fairfield Processing and Star Machine Quilting thread from Coats. Sample stitched on a Brother Innovis D sewing machine; machine-quilted by Dianne Hodgkins.

**Page 155:** Look at Me!—Sulky Variegated Rayon thread, Steam-A-Seam2 fusible web and Hobbs Fusible batting.

**Page 164:** Fish & Bubbles—Machine-quilted by Nancy Hughson.

# Photo Index

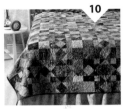

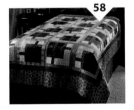

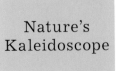

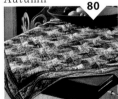

Falling Leaves **84**

March of
the Crabs **88**

Marvelous
Maple **92**

Under the
Apple Tree **96**

Happy
Scrappy
Living

Jacob's Ladder
Runner **101**

Autumn Stars **104**

Stars in the
Crossroads **107**

Tropical
Fish Mats **110**

Patchwork
Growth Chart **113**

Triangle
Illusions **116**

Love in
a Tangle **120**

Flowers in Bloom
Tea Cozy **124**

Patchwork
Bags

Scrappy
Sewing Pod **129**

Starfish
Beach Tote **132**

Wedding
Gift Bag **136**

A Denim
Beauty **140**

Little
Treasures
Baby Quilts

Cute as a Bug
Baby Quilt **145**

Hearts A-Flutter
Baby Quilt **152**

Look at Me! **155**

Choo-Choo
Baby Quilt **158**

Fish &
Bubbles **164**